Yours fatally,

Profitism

Gavin Sinclair

Gavin Sinclair was an academic psychologist, then an organizational psychologist in private practice. He has been meditating since 1986. He was radicalized in his political thinking and beliefs at the age of 20, since when his outlook has been modified into a blend of Western and Eastern knowledge and experience.

www.gavinsinclair.net

My father told me something I've never forgotten. You've got two forces in life that control everything. Just two. The Profit Motive and Human Values. Sometimes they run together but mostly it's war. Pick your side early, my father said, and stick with it. And by the way, my father said, remember this: the Profit Motive always wins.

A character in <u>The New Confessions</u>, by William Boyd.

CONTENTS

FIGURES

Yours fatally, Profitism

PREFACE

Become happy, Stay happy was focussed on the happiness of you and me, the individual. I demonstrated that God exists, that God exists within us as our deeper selves, that we cannot be truly happy without coming to know that inner Self and that the way to do so is through meditation. If you are put off by the idea of God, but feel sure you have an open mind, read that book before this one.

In this book I intend to demonstrate the truth of an equally unlikely, or at least in this sceptical and secular society, unacceptable hypothesis: that the current abysmal state of the world is directly and indirectly attributable to the historical and more recent excesses of capitalism. The old capitalism, which continues to wreak its customary havoc on the world, has now been joined by the new capitalism which is taking over the collective mind of the young.

Old and new capitalism must be curbed and their excesses eliminated. Many who can see what the Profit Motive has done and continues to do have either tried to work against it, or wish they could think of a way to do so. This book, relying on the acceptability of the conclusions in Become happy..., offers the only *potentially* viable solution.

This book is both a sequel to Become happy... and a companion piece. It is aimed at helping those concerned about the way the world is heading to see why and how things are disintegrating on so many fronts, and what each of us can do about it.

First, a quick overview of Become happy, Stay happy:

BECOME HAPPY, STAY HAPPY

Recapitulation

God exists, and for whatever reasons God has, intervenes in our lives from time to time.

We desire a much stronger spiritual component in our day to day experience than we are aware of. This truth was demonstrated with the cooperation of the reader.

The desired qualities are divine, i.e., they are of and from God **.

God does exist 'out there', but far more importantly, God exists 'in here'. "You're God dwells within you, as you." [Swami Muktananda]

Religions are useful for charity and comfort offered, but are next to useless if we wish to know and experience our own inner Self.

Unless we make the effort to have that knowledge and experience, we will never be happy or contented.

Meditation is the only guaranteed path towards that goal.

** The Three Qualities

Indian philosophy and scripture distinguish three classes of experiences which may or may not be strongly present in any person or situation. These are thoroughly canvassed in Become happy... I have developed a questionnaire in an attempt to capture the essence of the three qualities as they affect us. In the questionnaire they are presented in randomised threes, with the instruction that the respondent choose between them – highest rank to the most important and desirable, lowest to the least, and a middle rank for the alternative in between.

Here are the defining characteristics for each quality, separated into their three categories.

The Three Qualities (by questionnaire)

*[See <u>The Bhagavad Gita</u>, Chapter XIV, where these qualities are named **sattwa, rajas and tamas**.]*

First Quality (Q1)	Second Quality (Q2)	Third Quality (Q3)
contented	passionate	stoned
joyful	successful	in luxury
loving	excited	lazy
fearless	aroused	unconcerned
generous	dynamic	be spoilt
peaceful	stimulated	uninvolved/ignorant
faithful	active	bingeing
insightful	energetic	partying
kind	achieving	self indulgent
cheerful	vigorous	stay 'cool'

These qualities will be referred to regularly in this book. As with readers of <u>Become happy</u>..., I invite you to consider which of these qualities you would prefer to experience most of the time. My underlying assumption is that in your honestest moments you are more attracted to Q1 than to Q2 (possibly vice versa if you're young), and a mile ahead of Q3. Yet many of us *live* in virtually the reverse order.

<u>Become happy...Stay happy</u> aims to help people turn that around and experience the happiness and love they miss and desire.

<u>Yours fatally, Profitism</u> invites you to expand the benefits of your growth in happiness and wellbeing, to add to infection of capitalism with the beneficial virus of love and compassion.

Gavin Sinclair

1 THE PROFIT MOTIVE AND HUMAN VALUES

Preamble

If you are a strong believer in the benefits of capitalism, and can see only minor disadvantages in the process, you could consider bailing out now. I would much rather you did not because the last thing I want to do is preach only to the converted. I don't want to 'prove you wrong': I want to persuade you that there is much more going on than you might be aware of. If I fail in the attempt, no harm done. I am confident you will at least be diverted, possibly intrigued, by some of the argument and evidence presented.

Need to create history

Olde Worlde people such as myself are inclined to bemoan that we live in a materialistic and Godless society. The current Western culture is not God-*less*, it is God-*denying*. There is nowhere God is not, so he has not abandoned us. He is waiting to see what we do with our free will, whether we can put in the effort to change the way we see the world's opportunities and the things we want within and from it. Since it is clear that present beliefs and practices will never achieve these desires, we must do something else, we must deliberately create history. Try this:

> If you keep on thinking what you've always thought, you'll keep on doing what you've always done.
>
> If you keep on doing what you've always done, you'll keep on getting what you've always got.
>
> So, if you want to change what you get, you must change what you think and therefore what you do.

The human spirit

The human spirit is in great shape, except among the wealthy, the aspirationals and those hopelessly mired in Q3 (ignorance, inertia, violence). For the rest of us, until recently including myself, this spirit also rarely sees the light of day. Some months ago thousands of State Emergency Services volunteers, on a long holiday weekend, helped out with wind and rain-damaged houses and businesses up and down the coast. Just as thousands of volunteers come rushing to help with bushfires and wildfires. In addition to these selfless people, in our societies are many people and organisations working to advance Human Values. They struggle against the might of corrupt and indifferent politics and corporate indifference and greed, and do the best they can. All these people set a wonderful example for the rest of us, as is warmly corroborated by corrupt politicians and corporate apparatchiks, who are more than happy to praise and to leave all life-advancing work to others.

I am going to sidestep these selfless and dedicated people and groups for one reason only: they are and must remain ineffective in challenging the power structures which control society and the world. The do-gooders – to use the sickening term of contempt used by the do-badders – must, perforce, work within the world as they find it. I am not one of these people: I do not have the courage, the dedication or the perseverance. But I do have the luxury of seeing the whole game, from which outlook I will now outline Western societies as they are, starting with the nature of our politico-economic system.

Human values and society

Australia used to have what was known as a mixed economy, where major infrastructure – roads, hospitals, public schools, universities (in Western Australia a university education used to be available to matriculants completely free), telecommunications, postal services, air, rail and bus transport, etc – were provided via public funds, with capitalism making its money from all the remaining activities – banking, insurance, retail, manufacturing and so on. No longer. The quickly growing trend is away from any notion that a society is responsible for looking after its own, to one of user pays to generate profit for the provider of each and every service, even, perhaps especially, the most essential, power, water, shelter, communication.

There will always be entrepreneurs; they can spring from any occupational source and until recent times were often beneficial to society. In the 1960s I knew of a butcher in Canberra who made a fortune by giving away butchering and moving into production and sale of butchers' paper. I know a woman who was a doctor's receptionist and started a company to train women who wanted to get such a job. The demand is there and the company is expanding. All such star-following should be encouraged. Most people lack these skills, however, and must coordinate their lives in some other way.

John Lennon's overrated song, *Imagine*, invites us to indulge fantasies about the potential elimination of human nature – greed, power hunger, and susceptibility to superstition, propaganda and, at least in the US, sentimentality. Some mix of these hurdles has held humanity back since *homo sapiens'* time began. I am not going to invite you to fantasise about a society where the Profit Motive lives in harmony with Human Values. It cannot do so. I am going to invite you to speculate on the possibility of a society which supports, defends and provides for its citizens, much as 'primitive' tribes look after theirs, and where Human Values can softly, softly catchee more and more influence.

To keep the search as realistic as possible, let's not focus on what a Human Values oriented society would be *like*: let us simply ask, what would it achieve? What follows here cannot be an exhaustive listing of Human Values. It is presented to highlight how far away from Human Values our society has drifted, and to pose the question, answered as best I can later, can this gap ever be closed, and if so, how? A society is oriented towards Human Values if it promotes and works towards, in no particular order:

A Human Values-oriented society would work towards:

emphasis on community

equality of access to the law;

equality before the law;

genuine efforts to diminish the effects of sexism, racism and ageism;

honesty and straightforwardness in dealings;

adequate food for all;

adequate shelter for all;

adequate and affordable health care;

fair educational opportunities;

security in employment;

equality of work opportunity;

caps on the fruits of greed and avarice;

respect for heritage;

unselfconscious and unforced encouragement of the value of love, peace, courage, generosity, understanding and empathy,

the experience of gratitude, goodwill; and

knowledge itself having intrinsic value.

...and would condemn and work against:

indifference to community, emphasis on the individual

inequality before the law;

sexism, racism and ageism;

dishonesty and sneakiness in dealings;

hunger;

homelessness;

poor health because of lack of funds;

educational inequality bred of wealth or lack of it;

unemployment and insecurity in employment;

excessive funnelling and accumulation of wealth, where this precludes exercise of the other values;

indifference towards or contempt for heritage;

hate and violence, cowardice, meanness in spirit and action, indifference to suffering, manipulation and exploitation for gain, ill will; and

the pursuit of knowledge only if it has immediately obvious practical value.

Why do issues such as these rarely enter the language of politicians, and never the spoken or written word of industrial and commercial leaders? If concepts, hopes, desires are ignored for long enough, and are never given credence or even mention, what must happen to them, particularly when there are strongly promoted competing ideas to take their place? They must wither and possibly die.

Given circumstances they consider appropriate, the movers and shakers swear to alleviate the world's problems, poverty, war, disease, climate warming. World leader summits end in an orgy of self congratulation and earnest pledges which, if recent history is a guide, will not be honoured. Surely humanity has the wit to come up with an approach which will seriously address issues such as these. Can we learn from historical efforts to improve the human condition? Over the past couple of hundred years, the citizens of earth have thrown up two very different politico-economic systems, designed to serve mankind. Can either of these teach us something? Certainly, each has been a spectacular spiritual failure.

Before we turn to these, here are the in-general choices currently facing Western societies ... and you and me.

Gavin Sinclair

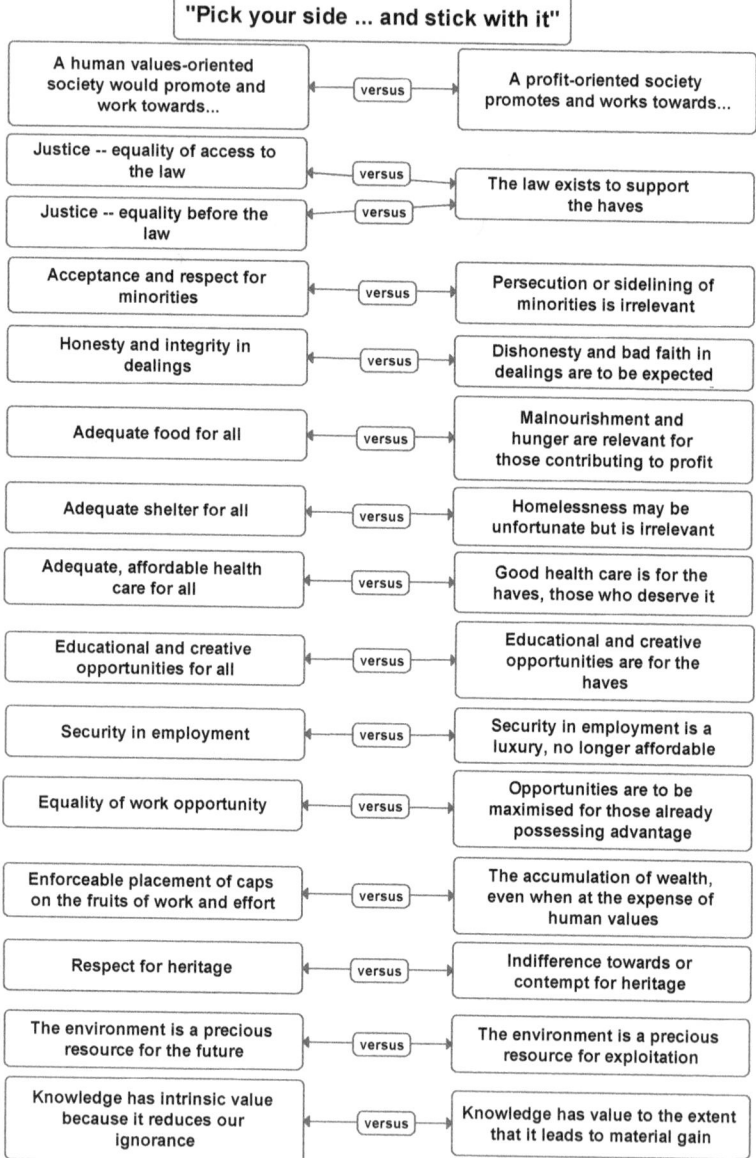

"Pick your side ... and stick with it"

A human values-oriented society would promote and work towards...	versus	A profit-oriented society promotes and works towards...
Justice -- equality of access to the law	versus	The law exists to support the haves
Justice -- equality before the law	versus	
Acceptance and respect for minorities	versus	Persecution or sidelining of minorities is irrelevant
Honesty and integrity in dealings	versus	Dishonesty and bad faith in dealings are to be expected
Adequate food for all	versus	Malnourishment and hunger are relevant for those contributing to profit
Adequate shelter for all	versus	Homelessness may be unfortunate but is irrelevant
Adequate, affordable health care for all	versus	Good health care is for the haves, those who deserve it
Educational and creative opportunities for all	versus	Educational and creative opportunities are for the haves
Security in employment	versus	Security in employment is a luxury, no longer affordable
Equality of work opportunity	versus	Opportunities are to be maximised for those already possessing advantage
Enforceable placement of caps on the fruits of work and effort	versus	The accumulation of wealth, even when at the expense of human values
Respect for heritage	versus	Indifference towards or contempt for heritage
The environment is a precious resource for the future	versus	The environment is a precious resource for exploitation
Knowledge has intrinsic value because it reduces our ignorance	versus	Knowledge has value to the extent that it leads to material gain

2 COMMUNISM AND CAPITALISM

There have been two major attempts to solve the challenge of organising society for the greater good of citizens.

Supply economy, as ideal

Supply economies rely upon the knowledge and wisdom of the leaders, whose job it is to ensure that each citizen puts in as much effort towards the common good as possible, and in return receives everything personally needed. This always leads to the greatest good for the greatest number. Such systems are usually called communism. The leaders decide what the population needs, and then ensure that these goods are produced, that is, are supplied. The system is excellent at providing work for all its citizens, although difficulties do arise around the issue of whether the labour is being most productively employed and focussed.

Cooperation

Everything is owned by the people as a collective. Supply economies rely on the cooperation within and between the goods-supplying organisations themselves, and between those entities and the citizens. With everyone working towards a common goal – and with all the citizens committed to the notion that the state, the collective citizenry, is more important than its component parts – the society develops towards perfection by progressively fine tuning supply to the needs of the citizens.

Supply economies in reality

Communism does not exist as a reality; it never did. The great historical downside of supply economics was that the rational basic assumptions came up against human nature, and against a ferociously hostile Western world, with all its tricks and pressures, and lost. It would have lost anyway without Western paranoia.

Specifically, the leaders developed enormous bureaucracies for their own self aggrandisement and power, and the bureaucracies lost touch with the people and with their needs. Most production was irrelevant to need. The mafia of leadership killed each other off in pursuit of more power, and cynically manipulated or eliminated large sections of the population to their own ends. The people became progressively hopeless and wretched, and eventually turned. End of supply economy.

Demand economy, as ideal

Capitalism is an economic system which relies upon demands from markets, that is, from you and me wanting things and buying them. In turn, this demand determines what is produced by those who have the money, the capital, to do so. So theoretically we demand things, water from a tap, electric power, all the things which are driven by electric power, and all the things, such as cars, paints and toothpaste, which are driven by or made from fossil fuels.

Then those with the money say OK, we'll make these things for you at a price that will make us enough profit to keep doing this. Plus a little left over to find its way down to those without enough money and for the overall benefit of society. This always leads to the greatest good for the greatest number. [Nothing wrong so far, if it doesn't bother you that the top 1% of wealth owners in the US control 24% of the wealth. After all, that leaves a generous 76% of the wealth for the other 99%.] Needless to say, we are entirely dependent on you folks to keep demanding things, so we'll give you a little help in deciding what you really need and want. We will call this promotion, advertising and marketing, and these will lead to consumerism, which is good.

Competition, and survival of the most appropriate

The challenge is, how can we decide which of the capitalists will be best at providing which products? Fortunately, there are two natural forces helping out here: one is called competition, rather like the competition for survival that underpins the theory of evolution. The other is called market forces. The competition must occur on level playing fields or it would be unfair. Then those who can produce the products at the lowest cost and therefore for the best price, will succeed, as they should. This is called free enterprise and is terrific for everyone, as people can compete for the best jobs in the various enterprises, which provides them with an aim in life. Whether this aim has been fulfilled is measured by the number and value of things each person accumulates. Maximum accumulation provides and indicates maximum meaning in life.

Demand economies in reality

Citizens are coldly manipulated into wanting and then buying things they do not need by an increasing number of large cartels whose legally enforceable reason for existence is to produce profits for the relative few who own them. Most citizens have to make do with bread and circuses – junk food, sport, things, television and the world wide web.

Communism, Socialism and Utopianism

OK, there's the thumbnail sketches, now for a bit more detail, disposing of communism first. I bracket these three because, although they differ markedly in means they seek similar ends, which can be summarised in the excellent Aussie phrase: a fair go for all. I will be dealing with capitalism at length, and feel I must at least address the failures of communal ownership and control to provide a fair go society. Relevance to God will become clear later.

If you read Marx's *Communist Manifesto*, you will be a cold fish indeed if you are not moved. Unless you are committed to 'take as much as you can, give as little as you must', there is strong human value appeal in 'from each according to his ability; to each according to his need', which to me is the core of all versions of communism and socialism. Yet mankind's commitment to and experience of these systems has been disastrous.

Lord Acton, in pointing out the capacity of power to corrupt, was correct on more fronts than he realised. The ruthless power hungry always come out on top because power is one of the acids that dissolve good intentions, even when a reasonably idealistic left is in charge for awhile. On the rare occasions that human-values people do get into power, even they become corrupted enough to lose their power for doing good, and such good intention as may remain is soon corrupted by those who surround them.

If the powerful and influential look like staying principled, and maintaining their concern with Human Values, the right destroys them – Zapata, Lumumba, Allende, Guevara, the two Kennedys, Martin Luther King Jnr, Biko, even our own Whitlam, though he was allowed to remain alive, and in any case was as much undone by his own hubris as by outside influences. There are no recent examples: the right rules, OK? One brief exception: Nelson Mandela, whose beneficial influence has faded, reduced not by capitalism but by the corrupt and the power-hungry now in charge of South Africa.

Many attribute the failure of communism and socialism to base instincts, original sin, specifically the desire for power and wealth, seen as undermining all positive and good efforts. The 'you'll never overcome human nature' view. That was my opinion. It now seems to me more likely that the reason such approaches to solving the problems of the human condition have failed is the hubris at their core – excessive pride in man's capacity to act alone.

So I am not going to waste time on communism, communalism, socialism or utopianism. I am sympathetic with their aims. Their means have universally let their aims down. They have failed, and must always fail for so long as they repudiate God, and for however long capitalism is left unchallenged. I have never supported communism, and must now withdraw support from socialism and communalism. Alas, I must also remain indifferent to the idealism of the young. It is always ineffective and becomes more so, assuming it remains, as the individual grows older.

Gavin Sinclair

3 RADICALS OF LEFT AND RIGHT

Left wing radicalism

It is sad to watch a group of old lefties reliving their glory days - i.e., the days when their idealism was acceptable because they were young - and continuing to swear true allegiance to ideas which no longer apply to the real world. I am not saying individualism rules, OK, and therefore we have to fall in with it. I support Human Values, wherever found and however supported, but they are without value unless somehow rendered effective.

Once powerful, the historical left wing as a force in politics and politicians is spent. This is often interpreted as the triumph of the right, particularly following the abject surrender and collapse of communism. A current, reasonably apolitical opinion is that the left is now an anachronism because the working class, aspirationals all, has moved up into the middle class, and therefore does not need protecting from exploitation by the nasty capitalists. Everyone is now, or soon will be, a shareholding, home owning mini capitalist, blessed with all the benefits of a demand economy. This is true in the sense that the working class no longer sees itself as downtrodden and exploited, but this is because it is no longer downtrodden, merely exploited along with everybody else.

Now that capital is completely in control of the vast majority of sources of information and interpretation - schools, universities, media, etc, but particularly the media, the manipulation and exploitation of the citizenry is not recognised because everybody's in the same boat, yielding up their independence of thought and action. In a society of deaf people there would be no concept of sound. In a society marinated in greed and self interest there is no effective concept of justice or fairness.

Having staked out its ground and raison d'être, the left has been rendered either irrelevant or dreamily idealistic. A spent force or a non force.

Conservatism – in three Acts

And so to the right, but not, initially, looking directly at capitalism. Although capitalism and right wing ideology are very close bedmates, many on the so called left share much of right wing ideology. Right wing Hitler was a fascist. Communist Stalin was a fascist. Chambers of Commerce can be fascist lite. So are many union officials.

C1   Conservatism has three meanings. The first, opposed only by anarchists and fellow wackos, refers to the desire to see the retention of everything of value which has come down to us over the years and the centuries. Most people, including a majority in what remains of the left in Western countries, accept this conservatism as good, as being worthy of support. Conservatives of this mould are ready to examine the weaknesses and unfairnesses which abound in present systems, and to consider ways of changing or removing these. Let's call this C1.

C2   The second form of conservatism, C2, concerns itself with a narrow range of behavioural matters, most of which involve sexual or pleasure-oriented behaviour. Devotees of C2 tend to have strong fundamentalist religious views, and currently their main object of attack is homosexual relationships together with their offshoot issues, acceptance, rights, marriage, ordination, etc. More generally, C2s focus on opposing 'immorality', covering all forms of bodily indulgence and pleasure. Only C2s restrict the notion of 'immoral' to what people in cooperation do with bits of their bodies. They are politically powerful, more so in the US than in Australia or the UK. Politicians frequently pretend to support such extreme views because they are too frightened to oppose them in case they are seen to be immoral, and in order to attract the votes of the C2s. Currently, C2s are becoming, as they do over abortion, aroused in their opposition to embryonic stem cell research. They remain indifferent, however, to all other forms of life taking and otherwise bestial behaviour. Their righteous focus is a micron wide.

C3 The third conservatism, C3, is different from either of the former two, although most C2s are also C3 in orientation. C3 shows itself as an automatic, fear-and-anger fuelled stance against any change at all to the way things are now, or were until recently. People of this orientation are called reactionary; they react against every suggested modification to current practices, power relationships, law, custom and so on. Very few such people proudly acknowledge their routine opposition to every potential or actual advancement in Human Values over profit.

The issues on which they 'stand up' are not necessarily of earth-shattering importance. Think of the fluoridation of drinking water supplies, sloppy dress, liberal education, too much welfare for the unemployed. The vast majority of C3s, including most right wing politicians, vigorously pass off their rigidity and bigotry as being nothing more than an example of C1, desiring only to preserve the good and the valuable.

C3s, always wrong and always triumphant

On truly important issues the C3s are, in the fullness of time, invariably proven wrong. We have a beautiful example unfolding as I write, global heating, no, global warming, no, climate change, no, minor climatic adjustments representing nothing more than an example of the natural cycle of things. The C3s' current position at time of writing is yes, there does appear to be something which could, at a pinch, be called global warming, but the leftist scare-mongers, for ideological reasons, have vastly exaggerated the likely effects. We really have very little to worry about and anyway, actions to reduce, well, not the looming threat but the possible inconvenience, would hurt the grand deity of all, Profit.

How many political and commercial leaders have you heard over the years condemning and ridiculing those who were warning of an impending environmental disaster? I will not insult you with a repetition of the ways in which global warming is blighting and will blight the earth, its societies and cultures, its people, animals and plants. What I want to emphasise is that this is no more than the latest in an eternal-seeming cycle of stupid, blind, self serving and ignorant adherence to the latest disaster. Until now, the two recent most profound examples of the same phenomenon have been the wars in Vietnam and Iraq/Afghanistan.

There is now only a hard core of true believers who say the Vietnam War was a justified holy crusade against the sweeping advance of communism. Many of those who opposed the war from the start, and who were dismissed as communists, traitors, saboteurs etc, have never received the nod they were due, and such people, and the truth of their position, are never acknowledged.

The reason for this is that most forms of media are owned and controlled by psychopaths or C3s. These people ensure that the abject failure of the latest C3 cause, whatever it may have been, Vietnam, Iraq, is quietly shelved and forgotten, and is quickly replaced by a new Vital Threat and Danger to World Order – to the supremacy of capital – currently, militant Islam. So the C3s quietly lose on Vietnam, then gloriously rise on Iraq, then (now) lose on Iraq and Afghanistan while trying to oppose 'panicky and extreme' approaches to stopping global warming, now also being lost by them as a cause. They are far more frightened of the possible effects of doing something about global warming than they are of global warming effects themselves.

The relatively short time lapse between the Vietnam and the Iraq and Afghanistan wars means that many who vigorously supported the former are still alive and until recently were in power, champions of the latter, plus, they can breathe new life into themselves over global warming. They are incapable of learning from experience. They happily carry the flag from one disaster to the next.

Global warming

Probably the greatest example thus far of ideological conflict will be over who should do what about global warming. In the face of the greatest threat to life as modern man has known it, we helplessly watch the capitalists and their politicians line up against any action that would reduce shareholder value. You see, that's the whole point: they are not only reactionary and ignorant, they're insane. No crazier, of course, than the coal and oil supremos who are fighting every move to reduce CO^2 emissions. Why is it so? Why does God allow these people their influence and power?

He is waiting for us to wake up to ourselves and do something about it.

Right versus Left

One mistake liberals and left wingers make is to assume that those in charge on the right, who follow the Profit Motive clutch of activities at the expense of Human Values, are willingly going against values they know are superior to those they put into effect. The left is convinced the Dick Cheyneys and Tony Blairs and John Howards of this world are choosing evil over good. Yes they are but, Cheyney excepted, they don't know it, or are only dimly aware of it. This is *their* insanity.

To Human Values such as love thy neighbour, compassion, generosity, forgiveness, peace, they are genuinely tone deaf. Their radar simply does not register Q1 events or experiences. They may, from time to time, say the right things: our previous political leader, an utterly convinced economic rationalist and global warming denier, asserted that the economy has no value in itself, but only to the extent that it improves the lives and lot of the citizens. I don't know who wrote that for him, but he was singing a song that to him was without melody or meaning. The left should not expect to win the right wing over. The far right cannot adopt Human Values because they genuinely don't know, cannot *feel*, what they are. As God is meaningless to us unless we experience him, so Human Values provide an unknowable and unbeckoning pasture for our power brokers.

The left hate the right, not so much for their views, which to a Martian would appear marinated in hypocrisy anyway, but because of the things they do in pursuit of their own interests, while pretending they act for the common good. I don't know how many times I have heard politicians on the right assert that they act only "for the benefit of the Australian people." They then act like true right wingers, in the service of those with whom they identify, the already wealthy and powerful.

The right hate the left, not because of what they do, which is little enough most of the time, but because of what they believe. The right hate opposing views, can't stand them, as totally as fundamentalist Muslims of different persuasions hate each other. The hate is white and pure, unalloyed by any tincture of saving grace in the 'other'. Similarly, the right acknowledges no sliver of positive or well meaning motivation behind any and all statements in opposition to their own beliefs. You want fluoride put in the drinking water? That's because you don't care if you poison the children. You oppose the Iraq and Afghanistan Wars? You want a Saddam back in power, you want Al Qaeda to win. You want to give more money to the poor and desperate? You must know that would bring the economy to its knees, as well as encourage indolence. You want to stop the permanent destruction of our forests? You don't care about jobs; I thought you were supposed to care about jobs.

The middle 40%

Have you not noticed that, no matter how brilliantly exposed are the outrageous lies and divisive assertions of fascistically inclined politicians, thirty per cent of the population still believes and supports them, lies and politicians both. Another thirty per cent automatically opposes all right wing excesses. This leaves forty percent between the extremes, between the thirty per cent in support and the thirty per cent of opposers. As the lies become progressively exposed, the forty per cent in the middle gradually wake up and move in the other direction on the issue. Then the left, if in power, makes a mess of it and the middle forty per cent swing back the other way. This is why politics lurches from right to left, and back to right again when the left have botched things because they are hopeless managers, or the right has found a new fear to monger.

The essence of the difference between right and left is found in any political demonstration, in the clash between idealistic, naive, university youths and girls and the cops who harass and bash them. The educated, naïve, dilettante versus under-educated, brutal power. The police exist to protect property and wealth, and those who possess them. Such good work as they do is ancillary activity. This is the way the Western world, or at least Australia, works. Why is it so?

Conservatism and intelligence

Here may be part of the answer. Some years ago I developed a conservatism test, and ran it over a couple of hundred people, together with a little IQ test I have been using for decades. The correlation between the conservatism score and IQ was around   r = -0.50. That is, there was quite a strong correlation between being conservative and being less intelligent. And just recently I heard of a US study of right and left leaning students which found that the liberals were much more usefully flexible than were the conservatives, more able to adjust their behaviour as a response to informative feedback. I'd like to explore this further one day.

Of course it can't be that simple, can it? I recall one year having a hand in IQ testing all incoming freshers at the University of Western Australia. Those enrolled in Medicine had the highest mean IQ, followed by Physical Education students. Law students were down the averages and subsequently had a fair representation in conservative student societies, consistent with my hypothesis.

Yet here is an intriguing finding which I cannot explain: the Phys-Ed students were even more conservative in outlook, or rather, in inlook, than were the lawyers. Politically they did not look outwards at all, seeming to be interested in nothing other than their sport of choice and their bodies. Perhaps it is that non sporty conservatives are relatively less intelligent, while the sporty ones are merely massively indifferent to the issues that so engage right and left.

Don't confuse inclination with effectiveness

Left leaning people write letters to editors, take out full page ads etc, but most don't *do* anything. The right wing, being everywhere in power, does lots, including going to war for dishonest and corrupt motives, arming and funding fascist regimes and winning in the propaganda war against the left. It *looks* as though this is how things must be. The left is spot on but weak as piss. The right is wrong and strong.

4 HOW OPEN IS YOUR MIND?

My purpose is to highlight the excesses of capitalism in such a way that you will be persuaded to agree with both my analysis of the world's situation and my recommendations for steps towards a solution.

Before I launch into this in the following chapters, I want you to see the almost insuperable obstacles in my path, obstacles laid down in the minds of most of us. I want you to be aware of the extent to which you are likely to automatically play Devil's Advocate when confronted with my interpretations of world-wide problems and challenges.

Following are two path-choice tables, where I invite you to follow your path of choice down from top to bottom.

Abortion on request

First, here is the hackneyed choice:

> *A woman has the right to control what happens to and with her own body, &/or the ejected foetus is not a human being;*

versus

> *Every foetus has a right to life and is fully human. Abortion is therefore murder.*

Have a look at the following decision path. Keep in mind that, with a few minor adjustments, this chart could as easily apply to embryonic stem cell research.

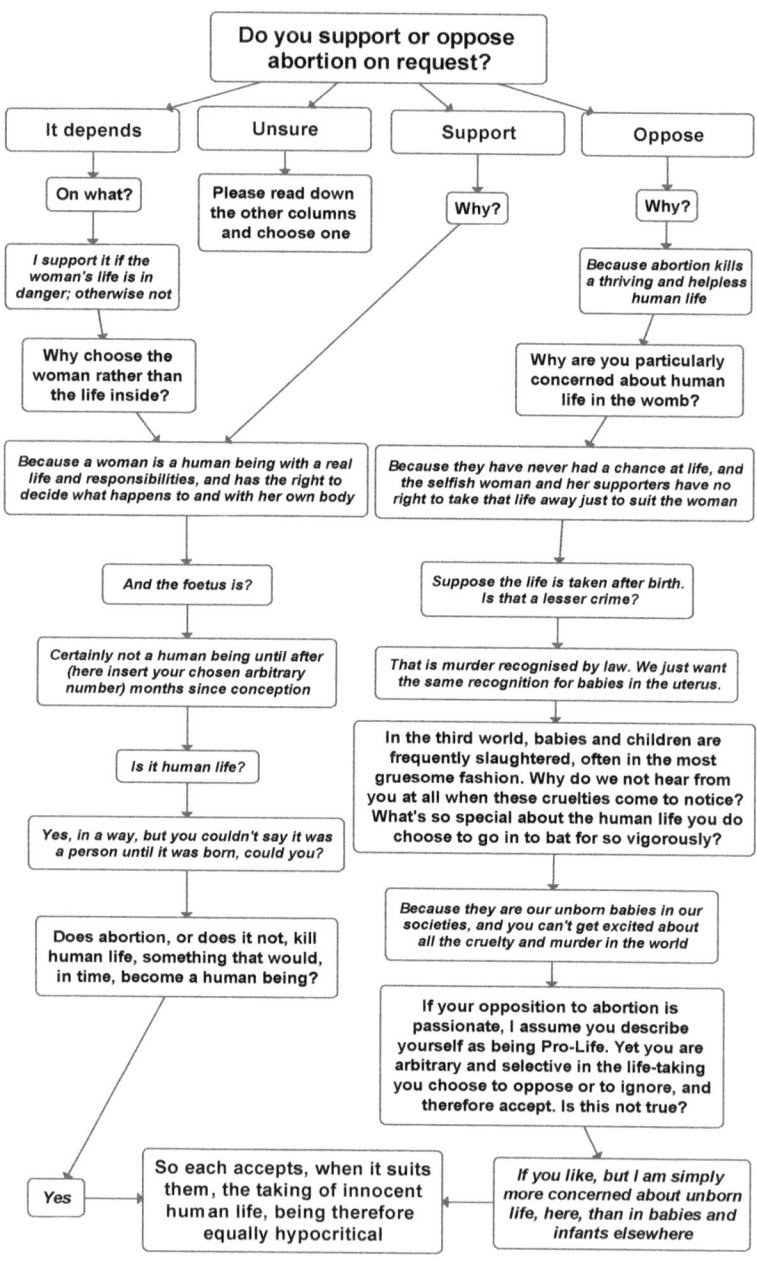

Re abortion on request

My own position is that given the worldwide indifference to the sanctity of human life, I cannot see why abortion is deemed to be such a special case. Abortion supporters could harness some courage and say yes, we are destroying a potential human being, but where the life of the survivor and its loved ones would be wretched in the extreme, abortion is the lesser of two evils. On the other hand, Right-to-Lifers could be a little less sanguine in the face of infant starvation, ill-treatment and needless death worldwide. Those supporting and opposing abortion on request are quite sanguine about human life-taking, so long as *they* can choose and focus on the circumstances under which life is taken, and the circumstances under which life-taking can be ignored, and therefore accepted.

9/11

Here is possibly the most divisive issue of our time, certainly so if we take a world wide perspective. Interpretations here completely separate the deliberately ignorant, the Islamic fanatics and the C3s from everybody else.

Gavin Sinclair

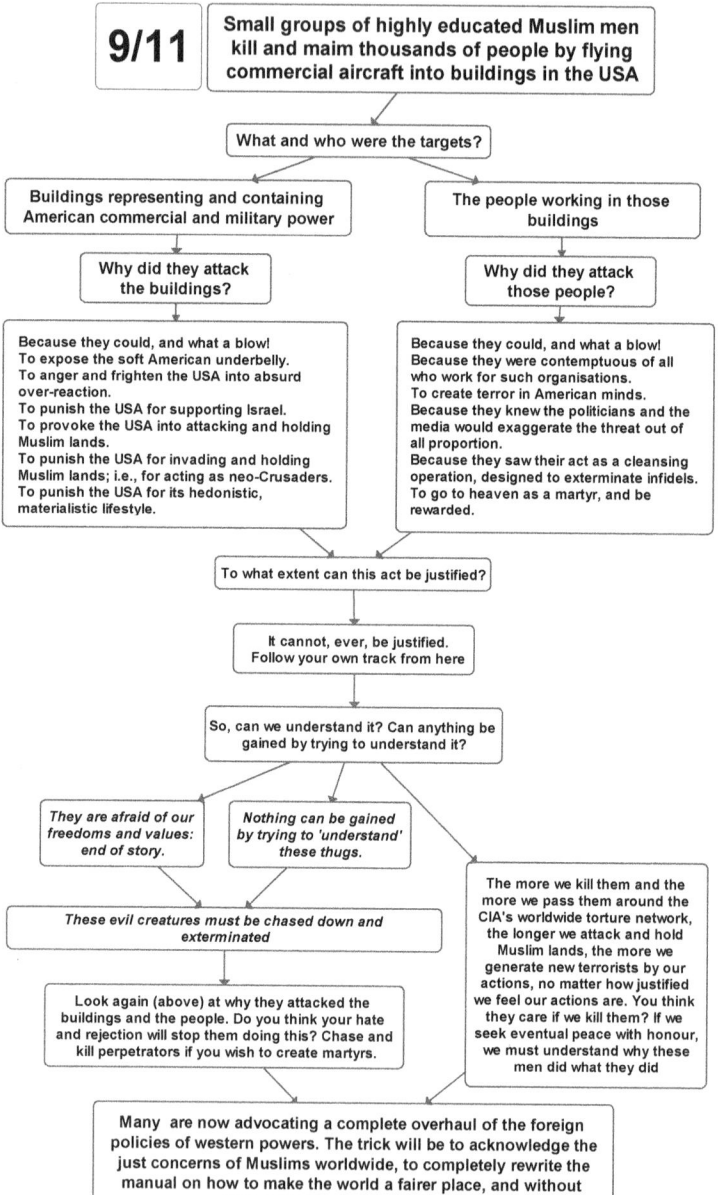

| 9/11 | Small groups of highly educated Muslim men kill and maim thousands of people by flying commercial aircraft into buildings in the USA |

What and who were the targets?

Buildings representing and containing American commercial and military power

The people working in those buildings

Why did they attack the buildings?

Why did they attack those people?

Because they could, and what a blow!
To expose the soft American underbelly.
To anger and frighten the USA into absurd over-reaction.
To punish the USA for supporting Israel.
To provoke the USA into attacking and holding Muslim lands.
To punish the USA for invading and holding Muslim lands; i.e., for acting as neo-Crusaders.
To punish the USA for its hedonistic, materialistic lifestyle.

Because they could, and what a blow!
Because they were contemptuous of all who work for such organisations.
To create terror in American minds.
Because they knew the politicians and the media would exaggerate the threat out of all proportion.
Because they saw their act as a cleansing operation, designed to exterminate infidels.
To go to heaven as a martyr, and be rewarded.

To what extent can this act be justified?

It cannot, ever, be justified.
Follow your own track from here

So, can we understand it? Can anything be gained by trying to understand it?

They are afraid of our freedoms and values: end of story.

Nothing can be gained by trying to 'understand' these thugs.

These evil creatures must be chased down and exterminated

The more we kill them and the more we pass them around the CIA's worldwide torture network, the longer we attack and hold Muslim lands, the more we generate new terrorists by our actions, no matter how justified we feel our actions are. You think they care if we kill them? If we seek eventual peace with honour, we must understand why these men did what they did

Look again (above) at why they attacked the buildings and the people. Do you think your hate and rejection will stop them doing this? Chase and kill perpetrators if you wish to create martyrs.

Many are now advocating a complete overhaul of the foreign policies of western powers. The trick will be to acknowledge the just concerns of Muslims worldwide, to completely rewrite the manual on how to make the world a fairer place, and without appeasing the murdering fanatics.

Re 9/11

I have provided my argument in the path-choice figure. If you cannot accept it, I cannot see you accepting very much of the following. Capitalism is responsible for the present state of the world. Add in tribalism, ethnocentrism, racism, etc, if you must, but trace all the major vectors back to their source and you will find it is some group wishing to exploit and profit from some aspect of the natural environment or of people. Capitalism's primary effects – unavoidable and growing disparity between the haves and the havenots, gross variations in opportunity for success, physical destruction of the world, etc – tend to mask the secondary effects: the cult of celebrity, sexualisation of children for profit, etc. We'll turn to these next, so we can then examine how such ... what, outrages? could possibly be part of God's plan.

The open mind

An open mind is not the same thing as a *laissez faire* acceptance of whatever comes along, a lily-livered weakness in the face of challenges to our own beliefs or expectations. An open mind is a curious mind, a mind that is unhappy about and suspicious of all ready-made, parroted explanations, a mind that is always pressing harder for a better clarification. An open mind is not challenged or offended by disagreement, even when one's most cherished beliefs and assumptions come under attack. All incoming information is taken aboard; it does not bounce off a sphere of ideological protection surrounding the mind and ego. An open mind is the best friend you can have for coping with today's crazy world.

5 OLD PROFITISM

Capitalism, to be called Profitism

No strong case can be mounted against those who succeed in capitalism so long as three essential conditions are in place: truly free enterprise, fair competition and freedom from market manipulation. These preconditions are, to all intents and purposes, never met. In the term capitalism there are no *intrinsic* implications that the allocation of capital can or will lead to disadvantage for anyone. So let's forget capitalism as a descriptive term – it is too neutral.

Consequently I intend to call capitalism Profitism, and those who work to advance the system Profitists. The first and minor advantage is that "Profitists and their spin doctors" doesn't have the same old left wing, hackneyed bitter ring as "capitalists and their running dogs". This, I hope, will get me away from the *sound* of clichés and platitudes, with the added advantage of focussing more on the motives than on the concept itself. The term communism correctly implies a system of economic and political control directed towards the interests of the community.

Profitism implies a system of economic and political control directed towards the interests of Profitists. Here is the essential Profitist precept:

Any activity which does not generate personal advantage is pointless.

Therefore only activities which yield personal profit should be undertaken.

The problem is not Profitism per se, nor those who make their living in and from it.

Profitism is like a scrub turkey digging up everyone's garden. It has to do what it does or it wouldn't be what it is. You aren't going to retrain it to stop scratching. Those who are caught up with Profitism, even those who represent the 'uglier' side of it, are merely playing out their role in the world, the role God has allowed them to adopt. They know not what they do, or if they know, they care not. As Popeye might have said, they yar what they yar. My desire and concern is to establish, once and for all and indisputably, that the world society, driven by and reliant on the Profit Motive, and relegating God beyond every pale, is becoming neither viable nor liveable.

A cornerstone of Profitism, constantly promoted by politicians and the spokespeople for Profitist institutions, is the notion of freedom of enterprise. As noted, this kind of entrepreneurship is on the way out. All useful or potentially useful commercial activities are being absorbed by corporations which convert them into profit centres. As fewer and fewer global corporations swallow more and more smaller companies and corporations, there is progressively less enterprise being permitted. For example, this drift towards fewer and larger corporations, together with the shift in power from creative people to money people, is the main reason Hollywood movies are so tediously similar. Accountancy *über alles*.

Genuine enterprise under threat

There are two strands to this crushing of individual enterprise: by gobbling up more of the market the biggies leave less room for innovative enterprise outside their own borders. When an entrepreneur challenges some area of the corporation's own offerings, they are either bought out or destroyed. Currently, most successful entrepreneurial activities have to do with extreme sex and violence, particularly as offered on the web. These contributions to our culture have not yet been corporatised but soon will be, just as soon as society's values and expectations have been sufficiently degraded to allow corporations to do so without undesirable backlash or loss of reputation.

The corporation as person

In the nineteenth century the owners of capital in the US did one very clever thing. They managed, through their control of legislatures, to ensure that companies and corporations henceforward were to be treated, legally, as though they were living beings. They must therefore be accorded the protections available to the USA's citizens. Australia has adopted this corporation-protecting legality. Managers and directors must act to protect and increase shareholder wealth. They cannot act against shareholder value or interests, no matter how the other stakeholders may be disadvantaged. Profitism therefore *must not*, except for marketing purposes, support generosity, empathy, fairness, equity, life itself. It was and is OK for the owners to do so if, as individuals, they felt so inclined, but the *responsibilities* of the corporation's executives were and are to the owners alone.

It follows that the Profit Motive cannot permit Human Values, because money spent in the service of Human Values would diminish the profit outcome sought. A perfect example of this has been occurring in Australia recently. With a view to undermining the union movement, the recent Commonwealth Government introduced legislation requiring individuals to negotiate a workplace agreement with their employer, with the legislation permitting the employer to abolish previously universal benefits, such as overtime pay for overtime work and sick leave entitlements, without compensating pay increases. Thus in one stroke the Human Values supported by such benefits (more time with family, reduction in financial worry due to sickness, etc) were eliminated in favour of greater profits for employers.

This introduces another feature of right wing government action in support of profit: profit-related legislation tends to be so blatantly one sided when first introduced that when they are forced to retract bits of it – which in this case they were – usually because of public outcry, the legislation subsequently passes almost as originally designed. This is very clever, and gives the parliamentary opposition or genuine liberals in their own ranks a warm feeling that it has achieved something.

Banks

Modern Profitism is seen at its most elemental in the activities of financial institutions, the functions of which could not be further removed from Human Values if the world's geniuses set out to do so. The banks say they wonder why they are hated. This is tongue in cheek spin. In the year before the Great Financial Crisis, the banking cartel in Australia racked up $15bn in profit for the year.

When I left school my first job was with a bank for nearly three years. In those days service meant service. The bank loaned money at a higher percentage rate than it offered for investments, the difference between the two covering virtually all costs, with the excess comprising the profit margin, a handsome but not outrageous gain. They now make sure no bank breaks ranks and offers Joe and Jane Citizen a fair go, and blatantly siphon money from people's accounts in as many ways as they can dream up. They call this fee for service. What makes this super obscene is that banks produce nothing of value, they simply shovel money around, making sure every third shovelful stays at home.

I was aware, while typing that paragraph, that the flavour of modern bank ethics reminded me of something from my past. Now it has come back to me. I recall in my Byron Bay days, a local hippy community regularly held an exchange market. The understanding was that if you wanted something that was on offer by an individual, you offered for it something of your own that was of approximately equal monetary value and was of interest to the other person. One day a young woman was approached by a weedy youth with a see through beard who indicated that he wanted a beautiful shirt she had made, complete with hand crafted embroidery. He asked how much it cost, and she told him this was an exchange market, and gave him a quick rundown of the terms and conditions. He bent down, picked a dandelion flower, and offered it to the girl in exchange. In that subculture a flower was above price because alive and natural and beautiful. She, crying, was forced by the logic of the hippie market to accept the exchange, and the guy, smiling, walked on with the shirt. I hope he drowned.

With comparable morality the banks offer a myriad of miniscule 'services' for which they charge fees fifteen or more times greater than the cost of providing the facility. Currently, if you carelessly overdraw an account and quickly rectify the oversight, the bank enters a minus sign, to the left of your balance, and automatically prints an up to date statement which is mailed out for your perusal. [Since I wrote that, they don't even bother with the notification.] Total cost of the two automatic actions, less than $2. Fee, $30. Profit, 1,500%. [Item in the *Sydney Morning Herald* online, today, 18 May 2007: 'Customers have paid more than $4 billion a year in bank fees for the first time, with penalties for breaching bank rules the fastest-growing source. The average person now pays about $200 a year in fees.']

Private equity buyouts

Am I being unfair to the banks? Is there an even more parasitic Profitist activity? Well stap me, there is. For some time now Australia has been for sale. Cashed up and usually overseas owned private equity companies and groups of companies – where did they get their uncountable money? we'll never know – with expertise only in asset stripping and corpse selling for the profit of shareholders, are buying up long established, large Australian companies. This trend is certain to continue, whichever political party is in 'power'.

Sometimes these predators pretend to expertise and interest in the target company or the industry in which it operates, but this pretence is quickly and cynically revealed after the deal goes through. So we are no longer subject only to large corporations getting larger by swallowing erstwhile competitors – called mergers to divert attention – we are now yielding the nation's birthright to organisations which have no goal whatsoever other than to enrich owners. That is, the men and women who own these marauders and the institutions which have large holdings in the marauders increasingly determine how and where the world will head. And why? The why is to make them personally even richer, without having to do anything other than make themselves personally richer.

Profitism and Faust

If you commit totally to the values and goals of Profitism, you are rejecting forever enlightenment or spiritual realisation, along with the First Quality experiences of generosity, compassion, kindness, thoughtfulness, courtesy, unconditional love, a fair go. These are not only absent from excessive Profitism, they are anathema to its basic ethic. If you commit to, or even passively accept, the demands and rewards of Profitism, you *are* sacrificing your soul. Q. What is wrong with: 'There's nothing wrong with the Profit Motive.'? A. It dissolves and replaces all Q1 desires with Q2 dreams, motives and actions, which usually degenerate into Q3 indulgences.

Only in a Profitist culture could works of art be bought, not because the purchaser *likes* the thing, but solely as an investment or as a status object. Only in such a society could rates of suicide, obesity, global warming, etc, be ignored until someone comes up with the real cost to the society, in oodles of $$$s in lost production, or in massive health expenditure. As Christ was tempted by Satan, so are we all tempted by the lure of the well named holy dollar. Surrender to me and you can have the biggest McMansion in the gated community, all the bodily pleasures you could possibly want, the absolutely best of everything. Travel to every exotic corner of the world and protect yourself from local contamination by staying in identical six star hotels all the way. All the dollar asks, along with the God of the Old Testament and of the Koran, is that you attend to, are attracted by, worship and obey no other god.

Capitalism China style

A relatively new wrinkle in Profitism is being developed by China. Pay whatever the Westerners ask for the needed building blocks, iron ore, coal, essential minerals, brains, then make them feel good by letting them come in to have a gobble at the trough themselves. All the while, flood the world markets with absurdly cheap goods – everything from toys and clothes to clones of Western machines and machine parts – which may not be excellent, but which certainly do the job. By this means either destroy the manufacturing base and the economies of the client countries, by developing astronomical trade deficits to their disadvantage, or force them to come to China with all their expertise.

When the crunch comes, the only Westerners in China will be those happy to suck off the big teat at close quarters. By which time the non-Chinese economies will be truly stuffed, bankrupt, and wholly dependent on imports from China for everything they regularly want or buy. The Chinese then call in all debts, double all prices, and make the killing they have been aiming for all along. Very neat.

Let the market solve it

It is conventional wisdom that market forces can resolve all human evils and difficulties. Thus, the market is being invoked as the saviour of the world from global warming. Except in Russia after the collapse of communism, where the whole process was obviously and laughably corrupt, privatisation of public assets is justified by appeal to the infallibility of market forces.

There is a fatal flaw in this argument. Even if poor nations, or poor sections of rich nations, want and seek what the Profitists have to offer, what market force is apparent which will move those desirables from the supplier to the consumer? Where is the profit in selling to those who cannot afford to buy? What a load of crap. Profitism cannot convert the havenots into haves without becoming non-Profitism. Under Profitism it cannot, cannot happen.

Global warming and renewables

Similarly, Profitism cannot take the steps necessary to combat, reduce and eventually eliminate production of the gases which increase global warming. Too much money has been sunk into the current 'dirty' technologies. There are other significant contributors to the gas increases – animals farting, frozen peat bogs thawing, Indonesians and Brazilians burning their forests, etc – but the two main areas of human-generated gases are the burning of fossil fuels, particularly by vehicles, and the generation of electric power, also created by burning fossil fuels.

Take Australia. There is not the slightest doubt that we could, given determination and allocation of money and resources, convert our sunlight and winds into more power than we need. [In Seville, Spain, an 11 megawatt solar power station was opened on 30 March 2007.] In Australia, as elsewhere, there would be a need for massive funding to get it up and running and there's the rub. All current investment is in the non-renewables, coal and oil ... and possibly nuclear. Even if they saw a future in renewables, those with the capital feel they cannot drain funds from their current investments to invest the necessary amounts into the establishment of renewables. They have left it too late: the consequences of their insatiability and indifference to Human Values is upon us.

Non-renewables and ongoing profits

There is another problem for Profitists when considering renewables. With non-renewables they can keep selling the primary stock, oil, gas and coal, as well as making profits from the generation of the power thus made available. With solar, wind, wave and geothermal, the primary stock is free. They could make a profit from these only by blocking them and charging fees to make them available, which they would do if they could but they can't. Their best outcome would be analogous to the toll roads currently infesting eastern Australia's travel corridors. The people, through their taxes as allocated by the politicians, contribute large amounts of money to venture Profitists, who then build the roads and tunnels and thereafter forever charge greedy fees for people to use them.

That would work. Sink the necessary trillions into research, development and establishment of adequate renewables-based power, then overcharge for it for evermore. Alas, as I said, it's too late. Besides which, they won't do it, unless forced to do so, and who's going to do that? Ha!

A final word, on the mood, the atmosphere, the *feeling* of Profitism. This is nowhere better captured that in the popular old time game of Monopoly. The whole thing is quite fascinating. It sucks you in. Nobody said Profitism was boring. Winners become obscenely gleeful and unkind towards losers. The losers become furious, noisy, depressed, and manifest feelings of self pity and worthlessness. Under no circumstances do Q1 characteristics appear in any player. Monopoly is Profitism in a nutshell.

6 CONSEQUENCES OF OLD PROFITISM

The trickle down effect

'The "trickle-down effect" is a now-discredited theory of distribution which holds that the concentration of wealth in a few hands benefits the poor as the wealth necessarily "trickles down" to them, mainly through employment generated by the demand for personal services and as a result of investments made by the wealthy.

The term "trickle-down effect" was coined by Ronald Reagan in a speech in January 1981 in which he announced huge tax-cuts for the wealthy, the benefits of which he claimed would "trickle-down" to the rest of the population.'

http://www.marxists.org/glossary/terms/t/r.htm

The recent financial crisis has highlighted how empty that rhetoric was. Everyone *knows* that since its inception Profitism has had difficulty in presenting itself as other than a system for exploiting resources for profit with little or no regard for Human Values. Depending on our samskaras, upbringing and experiences, most of us approve and support such activities, oppose them with varying degrees of passion, or don't care one way or the other. You will know by now that I am an ardent opponent, but I will not bore or irritate you with yet another catalogue of all the things 'wrong' with these

41

practices. I am more interested in outcomes than in the logic underpinning the gouging.

Anyone with a Human Values orientation must be contemptuous of historical Profitism, where the money required for supplying goods or services is held in private hands, and allocated in such a way as to do nothing other than maximise profit. This form of Profitism is alive and very well with reference to goods, but recently became relatively sick in relation to services, specifically, the allocation of money itself by the banks. Already the signs are that this 'global crisis' was only a hiccup, quickly fixed with public money, thus allowing the greedies to return to the trough.

In addition, globalisation appears to be here to stay and grow, with more and more resources and power being concentrated into fewer and fewer hands. This is inevitable, being the natural outcome of players competing with each other in the one jungle. I will call these processes Old Profitism, as they have been with us for two hundred or more years, and continue to have effects such as those listed below.

Impacts of Old Profitism

Degradation of the physical world

Rising sea levels are already scattering the peoples living near sea level. This process is going to continue.

Because of human expansion, exploitation and heating, a distinct species of plant or animal now becomes extinct every twenty minutes.

Those who can do something about it are resisting doing so. See High and Dry, by Guy Pearse, Viking Press.

'Development', advocated and pursued by 'developers', is, with the blessing and support of corruptible politicians, killing heritage.

Degradation of the human physical experience

Millions of farmers must lose their livelihoods as the earth dries out. This has already arrived in Australia's main food producing areas in Victoria.

The 'free trade' the west is so keen on always carries caveats to ensure that the industries of the strong are protected and the economies of the weak are made vulnerable to cheap imports, thus sucking wealth from the already poor.

Fifty thousand people, mostly children, have been blown apart in post-war Laos by cluster bombs. The US has consistently voted against any move to outlaw these weapons. Why, would you say?

The pharmaceutical giants won't sell cheap product to the developing world, and the tobacco lovelies are falling over themselves to do so.

About half a million sex slaves are traded around Europe per year.

One hundred and twenty thousand children have worked as soldiers in Africa.

Excessive focus on profit generation and on winning

To require pre-school infants to start learning skills for future employment is control, propaganda and enslavement. Where is fun? Where is curiosity? Where is play?

Telstra's 1,000+ inbound call takers, nominally employed to answer and help with queries, are also set ridiculously challenging sales targets, and are fired if they don't meet them.

The growing definition of customer service is to persuade people to purchase what is furthest from their mind and which they neither need nor want.

Stock exchange indices and share price fluctuations, together with who's eating whom, are coming to overwhelm news services.

Utterly meaningless and un-interpreted daily and weekly fluctuations in share and currency indices frequently lead the news.

Help calls to Telstra are now timed out after ten minutes, with no capacity to call back to the same person.

Sports people do not play for fun, or to compete: they play only to win.

Through fun and play little children get it too easy. You can't start too early to maximise subsequent profit fodder resources. We are also reducing parental anxiety by giving their child the best possible chance of future employment, which should be the

conscious goal of every child from the earliest possible age.

The giant food chains Walmart, Woolworths, etc, control the lives and livelihoods of far too many farmers and other suppliers, just as China will strangle our economies when it judges the time is right.

Employers requiring total commitment as a cornerstone of employability is to control the lives of employees, no matter at what level they are employed.

Employers demanding overtime work, particularly without pay, are similarly controlling the lives of employees, no matter at what level they are employed. Until the financial crisis hit, thirty seven percent work overtime or extra hours, with about half doing so for no extra pay

Enough!! We all know this, and we either care and wring our hands, or don't care and return to our own pursuits and pleasures. Although these anti-Human Values phenomena are clear pointers to where Old Profitism is now taking us, they are not the only focus of this book. The Profitism that concerns me more is a new development, certainly post World War II, and primarily in the last couple of decades. It gallops onwards to the murmur of only a few muffled mumbles of protest. If we can do something about this New Profitism, we stand a chance of subsequently, or even simultaneously, reducing the negative influences of the old.

Gavin Sinclair

7 THE NEW PROFITISM

Picture a beautiful full page photograph I saw in a young women's magazine: young man and woman are running towards the camera along a wild beach front, hand in hand, long hair flying, abandoned to their joy and glowing with such delighted love you know they are experiencing a Self-to-Self moment. Caption: _When is it OK to ask for his hair stylist's number?_ The Profit Motive in the guise of joy manifest.

New Profitism is marked by a recently developed and far more insidious control over wealth than was ever dreamed of in Old Profitism. The New Profitists have learned how to control what the populace thinks, wants, must have and do, and how it spends its money. It achieves this multiple whammy by nothing less than thought control, which sounds crazily paranoid and conspiratorial, and which I intend to demonstrate.

Some changes since the 1950s

Here are some changes I have noticed over the past fifty years, roughly classified. They are in no particular order. I was going to cast them in the context of what it was like in the fifties, concentrating on how today's undesirable and terrible things did not happen then, or were rare and shocking. Then I realised younger readers either wouldn't believe me, or would think I had mentally painted the past in a rose wash. The 1950s were, at least in Perth, a period bedded in sexism, racism and parochialism, spiritually stultifying to the nth degree. Some improvements in these are to be welcomed – e.g., increased openness and acceptance of people who are different, and immigration-inspired culinary and cultural expansion.

What I will list, with their consequences, are some less desirable changes where you and I are now living with the consequences. I ask you to take my word for it that each of the following was either unknown in the '50s, or jaw-droppingly rare. What do these developments have in common? See what you think.

Degradation of the human social/spiritual experience

In the West, corporate paedophilia creates and exploits fear in preteen and teenaged girls, fear of not being beautiful and of not belonging.

In commercials and advertising layouts, very young girls are made to look as sexy as possible.

Kids can have little resistance to the movie and web-conveyed debauchery of all kinds.

Over 100,000 people are now homeless in Australia.

Poker machines are now in pubs as well as in clubs, and there is a move afoot to have them introduced into shopping malls. The addicted and the near-addicted cannot avoid the well placed temptations and are therefore under control.

In consulting firms, the profit-relevant obsession – sell, sell, sell - excludes many who would make a strong contribution from within their area of expertise.

Feelings of helplessness, hopelessness, despair, worthlessness and impotent fury are experienced and evidenced widely among the struggling havenots, and universally across the underclass.

More than four out of five people, in Sydney and Newcastle, suffer mental illness or have a family member or friend who is affected (report commissioned by Wesley Mission).

The rate of eating disorders among Australian teenage girls has doubled since the last survey in 2000. Twenty per cent of girls are now starving themselves or deliberately vomiting to lose weight.

One in four Americans watches a family member struggle with addiction.

Families are flying apart as 'work' takes component members to all points on the globe.

Couples are not marrying, and are splitting earlier, children or no.

Any politician who advocates a rational approach to the drug problem, as distinct from a zero tolerance, hard on drugs, war on drugs approach, invariably loses at election time.

Degradation of values and principles

Gambling, alcohol and drugs. Why are the first two almost universally accepted as OK or desirable in our society, and drugs likewise by the young, when they take us away from Q1 and even from Q2 into Q3 and nothing but Q3?

In the US the gun lobby is more powerful than are the Big Oil and Pharmaceutical lobbies. Americans own 240,000,000 guns.

The existence of Abu Ghraib, Guantanamo Bay and the CIA's worldwide torture network. The previous US administration legalised torture as a legitimate tool in investigations.

To the extent that Australia remains in lockstep with the US's foreign policy and actions it will suffer the rest of the world's dislike and mistrust.

The illegal sport of dog fighting is on an exponential rise in the USA.

In movies now, following the lead set on the web, sex and violence are no longer suggested, they are whacked into your face. We now have real instead of simulated sex. What comes next? What about real rape, real murder, real murder with torture, real serial murder, real child rape, hey, freedom of artistic expression at last. Snuff movies rule OK?

There are no personal relationships possible any more with big organisations – e.g. telephone menus leading nowhere you want to go; crude and unreliable voice recognition by telephone answering computers.

Neither banks nor customers feel any responsibility to each other any more. Neither is at all identified with the other. The same can be said of most large commercial enterprises and customers.

The best tickets for top acts are now frequently to be auctioned, thus being made available only to the rich.

Post modern arts are chaotic, grungy and ephemeral.

Greed, lust and self indulgence are being successfully promoted as essential Human Values. E.g., advertising which constantly emphasises "spoil yourself...you deserve it".

There is a current fashionable acceptance of anal intercourse, male and female.

There has been a serious decline in moral courage; buck passing in all our private and public organisations is rife.

It is cool to be dishonest.

People are increasingly less likely to take any responsibility for their own actions or carelessness; hence, the ridiculous rise in litigation and, therefore, insurance premiums.

"Universities in NSW are facing an explosion in the number of students caught plagiarising assignments and cheating in exams, with Law students the worst offenders at one big institution." Sydney Morning Herald.

Via the web, kids now have ready access to pornography, graphic violence and general nastiness, despite online filters.

Education, health, research and the ABC, once seen to be societal benefits and responsibilities, have until recently been eroded to enable privatisation.

Development of violent, aimless backlash

Because seven school pupils died in a short period from knife wounds, manufacturers in the UK are developing knife proof school uniforms. Now an eighth has died, with an 11 year old playing ball with friends gunned down by a 13 year old riding past on a BMX bicycle.

The violent behaviour exercised by the worst-off of the havenots has refocused fear in all communities, as indicated, for example, by ever more repressive policing policies and practices, and by the development of gated communities. No-one even *thinks* of possible causes underlying the original behaviour.

Yours fatally, Profitism

When taking the drug ice, people can go for up to six days without sleep. Common among users are road rage and the conviction that they are being chased by aliens or cops. The use of this drug is closely associated with unemployment, low education, lack of services and ghettos created by governments dumping people in high-rise slums.

In some Sydney suburbs, young people are hurling rocks at passing trucks and buses, with an announcement that one rock struck so ferociously it must have been hurled by a catapult or similar.

Women cannot walk in the streets at night with safety.

Bus drivers are refusing to travel routes where they are constantly punched or spat upon. Ambulances and ambulance officers have rocks hurled at them in some suburbs.

40,000 women and children in NSW 'escaped' from violence to a refuge in 2005.

Serial and multiple murders are now common, particularly those described in our media as senseless, pointless, random, etc.

Violent madness is around us everywhere, taxi drivers murdered to avoid paying a fare, students gunning down dozens of colleagues because they were not friendly or accepting enough.

Not a day goes by that we do not hear of someone being stabbed during a post pub fight. Alcohol's main effect is to dissolve our inhibitions, those aspects of conscience which keep lust and anger under control.

Road rage is being joined by customer and shopping and stand in line rage in dealings with any organisation where the customer feels poorly done by, banks, some big stores, government departments, Centrelink, etc.

Have you seen parents of six and seven years olds screaming abuse at referees of kiddie football matches, even punching them; screaming abuse at their own children for making a mistake or for not trying hard enough?

Men now frequently kill wives who leave them, and are almost as likely to kill their children if not granted custody.

One game played recently for fun on Sydney's North Shore, by well educated youths in their late teens, has been to slap old people, any old person, hard in the face.

Development of less violent or non violent disaffection

You can see how much the kids hate their jobs behind fast food and supermarket counters by their eyes – estrangement in full dress.

Eighty per cent of those who called in to radio station 3AW in Melbourne supported cops bashing suspects to subdue them, even when already subdued.

Nobody whistles any more.

Kids rarely skip any more.

How often do you hear an individual practising on a musical instrument?

Look at the faces of the people in public transport. Feeling alive? Happy? Look at the face of any young woman walking towards you, smoking, and notice the frown of tension and distraction.

Healthy people park their cars in spaces reserved for the disabled.

Hit and run accidents were almost unknown, are now common.

Road discourtesy, once rare, is now the norm.

Many drivers no longer pull over for ambulances.

Flagging and taking a taxi, having already booked another one.

When people call you in error they just hang up, rather than say sorry, I got the wrong number.

Increasing numbers of relationships once close are breaking down because the male partner prefers masturbating to internet porn to live sex with the partner.

Doing nothing effective about kids' access to the web.

Parents, distracted, no longer teach their children, and require of them, manners or courtesy. As for respect, Ha!

Parents are not bothered to have their children do 'the right thing': they just let them 'get on with it'.

Finally, something to summarise the whole drift (Sydney Morning Herald, 20 October 2009). In a review of the latest video games:

"A prominent children's lobby group is calling on the Government to review its decision to classify as suitable for 15 year-olds an upcoming video game that allows players to assume the role of a terrorist and shoot innocent civilians in an airport. .... Call of Duty: Modern Warfare 2, a highly realistic shooter title due for release on November 10, is one of the most anticipated games of the year, having already won a slew of awards and having received an **average rating** of 94 per cent from critics." [Bold and underlining in original.]

"... suitable for 15 year-olds ... role of terrorist ... civilians ... most anticipated ... slew of awards ... 94 per cent...". I rest my case.

How things were

Let's flip just some of these over to give you the other side of the story. No kidding, this was Australia in the 1950s.

Children were *never* used in advertisements except for 'wholesome' purposes.

There were no poker machines.

The now common eating disorders among the young were virtually unknown.

Alcohol and tobacco advertisements were used only to plug themselves and were not attached to sport at all.

No extreme violence was *shown* in movies.

Banks were courteous and helpful.

No kids carried knives.

There were no gated communities.

Women would not think twice about walking home at night.

Pub brawls were settled with fists.

People whistled, kids skipped.

Drivers *always* got out of the way of ambulances.

Road, shopping and telephone courtesy were the rule.

In short, we may have been bored, but we were not abandoning responsibility and trying to escape.

Yours fatally, Profitism

Anomie

Anomie is the term defining the state into which many, perhaps most of us have been reduced by the avalanche of Profitist influence. Here are some web definitions you will find if you Google *define: anomie*:

Lack of moral standards in a society.

Alienation or social instability caused by erosion of standards and values.

Apathy, alienation, and personal distress resulting from the loss of goals previously valued.

An experience where there is a crisis of meaning on a personal or group level.

The definition best fitting the common stress and distress so many of us experience is this:

The disorganization of social and personal values during times of catastrophic stress. [J.P. Chaplin, Dictionary of Psychology].

As my wife clarified for me, our lives are becoming increasingly trivial and superficial, no matter what goodies we have surrounded ourselves with. We feel it. We know it. And we feel powerless to do anything about it. How has Profitism engineered us to this point?

The following figure sketches how Profitism has achieved such an all-embracing, all-saturating impact on everything and everyone. And why do we stand for it?

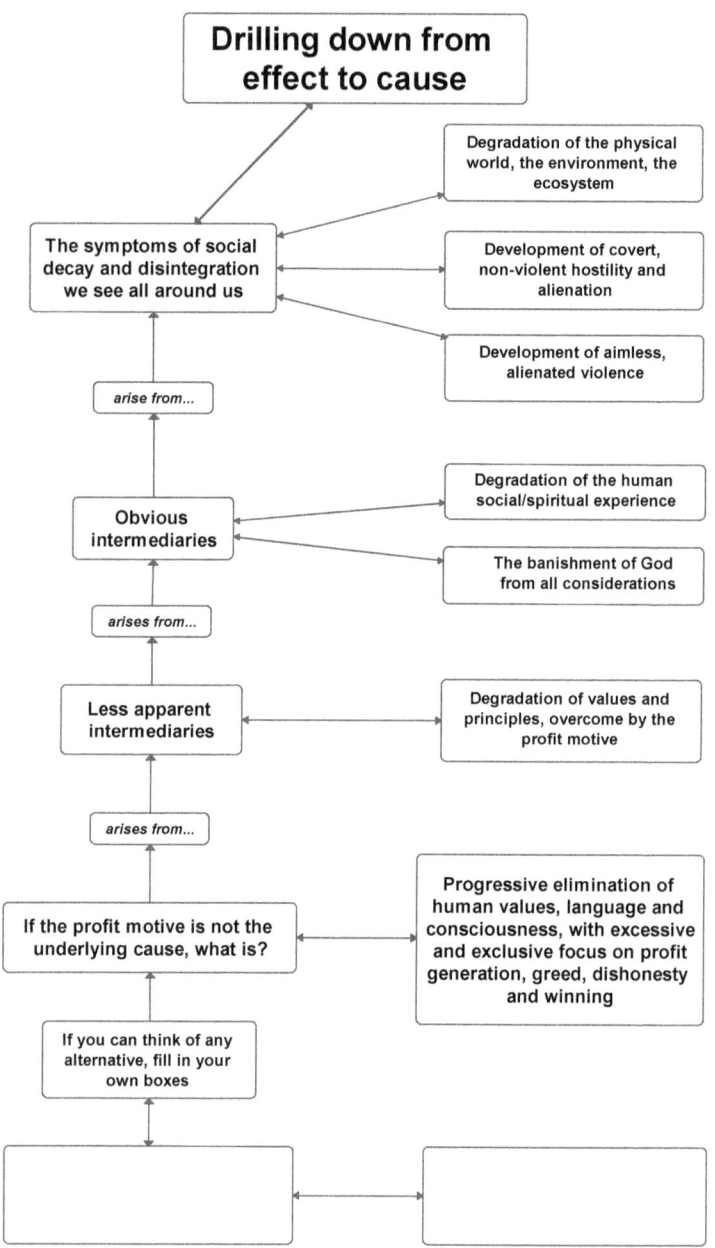

Gavin Sinclair

Drilling down from effect to cause

The symptoms of social decay and disintegration we see all around us

Degradation of the physical world, the environment, the ecosystem

Development of covert, non-violent hostility and alienation

Development of aimless, alienated violence

arise from...

Obvious intermediaries

Degradation of the human social/spiritual experience

The banishment of God from all considerations

arises from...

Less apparent intermediaries

Degradation of values and principles, overcome by the profit motive

arises from...

If the profit motive is not the underlying cause, what is?

Progressive elimination of human values, language and consciousness, with excessive and exclusive focus on profit generation, greed, dishonesty and winning

If you can think of any alternative, fill in your own boxes

8 ALIENATION

The many faces of alienation

When someone says, 'keep the music down, we don't want to alienate the neighbours', they mean don't anger or upset them, or put them offside. To alienate means to separate, to estrange someone from that to which they want to be close.

In his earlier writings, when he was a humanist and humanitarian and before he became a hardhead, Karl Marx wrote movingly and persuasively about alienation. I'll be brief because Wikipedia provides an excellent coverage. The most dramatic and far reaching example of the phenomenon in Australia has been the enforced alienation of the aborigines from their land. Our right wing politicians and historians scoff at this as being some sort of fairy tale, or at best a gross overstatement, but the aborigines spent 40,000 years becoming so identified with the land and the spirit world the land makes possible, that to deprive them of meaningful contact, to alienate them, as we have done, is to condemn them to death. Originally we dealt death with alcohol, disease and muskets. This occurred well into the twentieth century. Part of the aborigines' genetic uniqueness involves a low tolerance for alcohol.

More recently many have taken to petrol sniffing and drug taking. We can be sure the drugs are supplied by white people, as is the alcohol. We have destroyed their culture, their spirit and their bodies, then we sit back and bemoan how pathetic they are, drunk all the time, bashing their women, screwing little kids, unemployable most of 'em. And they die twenty years younger than we do. Well stap me! Just because we took their land away and poisoned them. Who'd've thought it?

Alienation versus satisfaction

Compare alienation with satisfaction. Marx uses for his example a person designing and making a fancy shoe, and then personally selling it to another who likes it very much and is pleased to make the purchase. For the period of design and manufacture the time spent on the shoe is the person's life, followed by the delight the manufacturer feels in the accomplishment and in the pleasure she/he knows has been experienced by the receiver. This person is realising his potential for joy and growth completely free from external demands or requirements.

Name me one job involving working for the man which draws on and gives free flight to the full range of skills and desires present in the job incumbent. Take a large sample of people in work other than self employment. Taking care to avoid surveying traps such as asking leading questions, ask the participants what they would work at if they had their druthers. Then ascertain what work they are doing now. For how many would the specified work activity be the same for both? Five per cent? Ten? Make an interesting study.

If one person starts up an enterprise as a sole trader, there is at least some opportunity to do exactly whatever would fulfil that person. As soon as the first employee is hired, Profitism enters. It is logically possible for the entrepreneur to recognise that the new skills are essential for progress, and to pay that person exactly the sum – assuming it could be worked out – brought in by those activities. So at least the entrepreneur would not be making a profit from the employee's activities. This never happens of course. The employee's input is charged out at more than it cost, leaving for the employer's profit what Marx called surplus value. But let's say full value has been paid to the employee. That person is still not doing exactly what they would do if they wished completely to fulfil their creative desires. Their output is still bent to the wishes of the employer. Enter alienation.

What it all comes down to is that Marx was right in analysis, wrong in remedy. Great physician, lousy surgeon. What we have is a society almost totally lacking connection between its component parts. Unless we work for ourselves doing what we like, we are all alienated from our work, and therefore from our true selves. We are becoming alienated from our families and from others. We are becoming alienated from the environment. When was the last time you walked in the bush? Finally, we are forced to be alienated from who we really are, because we must do whatever we would not do if the choice were ours, the basic curse Profitism has visited on us all.

Alienation and power

Not even the politicians escape. Look closely at a politician's eyes. They are not looking, they are watching. Then there are those who used to be liberal and progressive in outlook, and who were seduced by their very right wing leader into coming off the back bench into highly paid and powerful ministries. My wife noted that if you looked at their eyes when seen up close in a TV interview, when they mouthed the hard right line in their areas of responsibility, the eyes were flat, blank, as dead as their souls. Their success was their defeat, even if they were on $200K+ per year. The decisions they made, in defiance of their consciences did, in the service of the experience of power, strangle their sense of right and wrong. They became as alienated from themselves as is any drunk in the gutter.

Embedded alienation

Before leaving alienation, here is the most disquieting example of alienation I have recently come across. Forget brutal thugs, stones thrown at passing trucks, the graffiti plague, scratching the paint of new Mercs and BMWs, gang versus gang. In those contexts there is great anger and belligerency mixed in with the alienation. Recently I was driving behind an old Hyundai Excel hatch, with rear window wiper. The wiper blade assembly had been bent in the middle, upwards by 45 degrees. Such casual meanness, the behavioural antonym of kindness, speaks of a young man – try thinking of a woman doing that – completely free of Q1 experiences or contact. This individual was additionally burdened by a relaxed, automatic sadism which is completely unable to discriminate between perhaps worthy (Mercs, BMs) and certainly unworthy targets for the hostility. This is alienation at its worst, because it has dehumanised its victim-perpetrator. He is almost certainly beyond recovery.

Not you or me

You who are reading this book – unlikely to be among the hopeless havenots – please imagine yourself as someone who lacks all Q1 experiences, and then imagine how you might react to all the 'we are the most blest country in the world' claims by the highest in the land, supported by TV commercials, by all other advertising, and by the lying and bullshitting spin doctors who support the entire profit-serving mess. You think I overstate my case? Just look at the world around us. If you think everything is going just great, well, as finance guru Alan Kohler said in another context, I'd like to have some of the pills you're taking.

Listen to the words of those who, always for their own ends, mislead us. Watch the behaviour of those against whom the powerful preach, such as thugs and druggies, and tell me their behaviour is without justification and beyond our understanding. Every time something violent and terrible happens, the media and the spin doctors call the actions of the perpetrators mindless, pointless and so on. Yes they are, but I do wish the populist critics would add inevitable, which is so much closer to the truth and more informative for the rest of us. I may be a bleeding heart but God is not. He knows what is justified and what must be paid for later. I suspect we haves will have more to pay for than will the havenots.

The never changing populist solution

When a young person, or anyone for that matter, does something vile or violent to person, animal or structure, there is one thing of which you can be certain: their life has been completely free from Q1 experiences, and full of the Q3. Now that the eighth British schoolchild has been murdered, PM Gordon Brown is on the job. He is going to 'crack down' hard on the gangs. Another boil erupts and St Gordon brings all the forces of righteous power to bear on it – in rush the core cutters, the pus suckers, the hole scrapers and the skin scourers. If they're lucky no more boils will pop up in that area of skin for simply weeks and weeks. Populist politicians approach all problems as though they are skin deep, and the popular press sings their praises and demands ever more of the same.

Gavin Sinclair

9 THE YOUNG

Old man look at my life.
I'm a lot like you were.

Neil Young

I am particularly interested in the groups at either end of the age spectrum: the young, because they are the future, whether we or they like it or not, and the old, whose numbers are increasing exponentially, thanks to our health system, with its crazy priorities. First, the young. Generations X and Y have taken a smacking from just about everyone else over the past couple of decades, which has left them unimpressed. They argue that the current disintegrating state of society has been handed to them by the older generations, an argument difficult to refute.

Yet we are concerned about them and with good reason. One example of their current worrying behaviour is very much in the public view. A development close to the heart of parents is the rapidly expanding practice of binge drinking until more or less unconscious. In the following figure I sketch some possible reasons, underlying causes, which could account for this. My views are implicit in the figure.

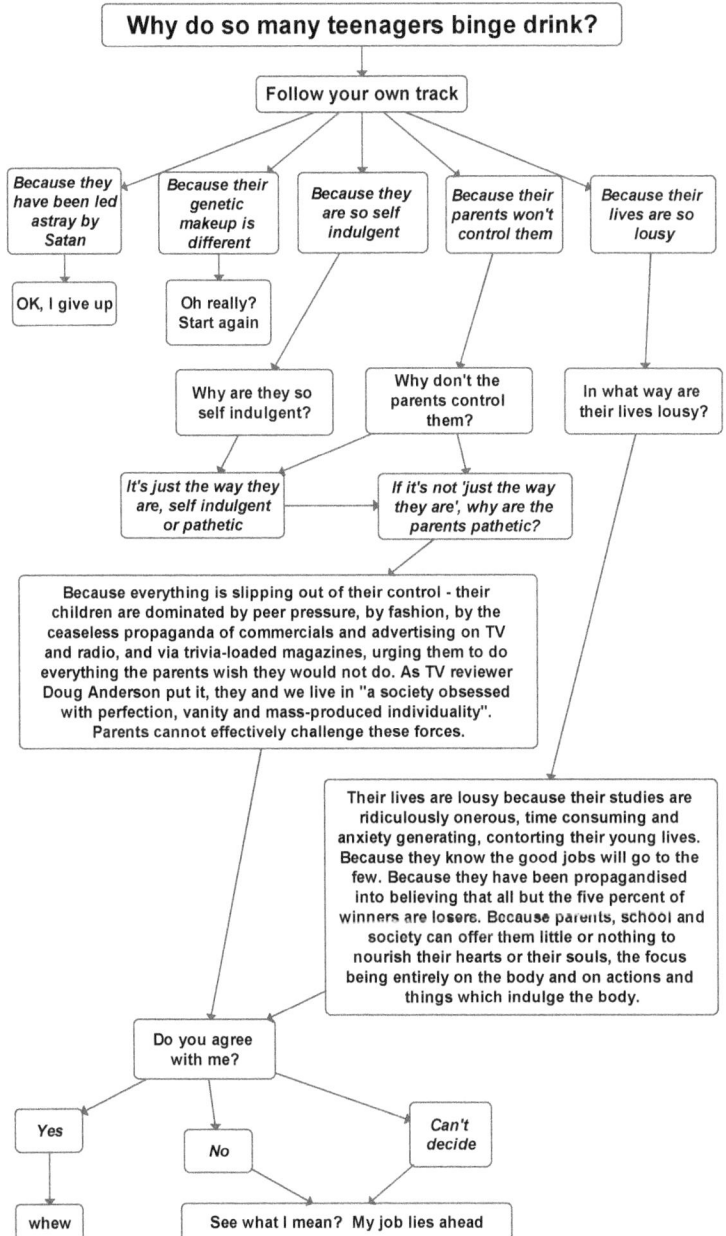

Why do so many teenagers binge drink?

Follow your own track

Because they have been led astray by Satan

Because their genetic makeup is different

Because they are so self indulgent

Because their parents won't control them

Because their lives are so lousy

OK, I give up

Oh really? Start again

Why are they so self indulgent?

Why don't the parents control them?

In what way are their lives lousy?

It's just the way they are, self indulgent or pathetic

If it's not 'just the way they are', why are the parents pathetic?

Because everything is slipping out of their control - their children are dominated by peer pressure, by fashion, by the ceaseless propaganda of commercials and advertising on TV and radio, and via trivia-loaded magazines, urging them to do everything the parents wish they would not do. As TV reviewer Doug Anderson put it, they and we live in "a society obsessed with perfection, vanity and mass-produced individuality". Parents cannot effectively challenge these forces.

Their lives are lousy because their studies are ridiculously onerous, time consuming and anxiety generating, contorting their young lives. Because they know the good jobs will go to the few. Because they have been propagandised into believing that all but the five percent of winners are losers. Because parents, school and society can offer them little or nothing to nourish their hearts or their souls, the focus being entirely on the body and on actions and things which indulge the body.

Do you agree with me?

Yes

No

Can't decide

whew

See what I mean? My job lies ahead

Gavin Sinclair

Stop Press *(Sydney Morning Herald,* 15 February 2010)

Jill Stark writes of Chris Raine, a 23 year old one time heavy binge drinker ("15 to 20 drinks a night most weekends") who, to the amazement and confusion of his friends, decided to give up alcohol for a year. He started a blog, *Hello Sunday Morning*, to document his 12 month experience.

Ms Stark writes: "On January 1, when his year of sobriety was up, Mr Raine found his desire for alcohol had greatly diminished. ... Through research conducted among his friends and the website, he discovered three main drivers of binge-drinking: a sense of identity that comes from being seen to drink the fashionable brands; a boost in confidence, acting as a social lubricant; and a way to deal with emotions such as grief, happiness or anger."

Thank you Mr Raine.

The symptoms

Adolescent binge drinking

Where the hell did the young get the idea that alcohol is not just for lubricating all sorts of fun but is for getting drunk as the aim of the activity? Could anybody young or old in their right mind believe that to get dead drunk is to be alive? To be temporarily dead is to be *alive*? Could such an absurd conviction exist without an underlying stratum of alienation and hopelessness? How far away is this from Human Values, however defined?

There would be very few people, aged between 30 and 110, who would not be concerned with the spectacular rise in the incidence of deliberately drinking till dead drunk by those whose brains and minds are still developing.

Frequently followed by wild brawling. What do you think is the underlying cause? And when you've decided that, how should those underlying forces be opposed and undermined, rendered ineffective?

Even more urgently, what can account for this genuine transformation in the role of alcohol in young lives? God knows I got drunk often enough in my youth and when I was old enough to know better. So did most of my friends and colleagues. Is the current generation of parents responsible, that is, are the parents now deliberately raising their kids to be alcoholics? It doesn't seem so, given that parents are among the most worried sections of society today, particularly with drugs energising the kids' booze. Perhaps there has been a frightful genetic mutation across Gens X and Y that turns them into booze guzzling, drug absorbing, violent or brain-threatened citizens. And perhaps not.

'Alienation and hopelessness'. Give me a causal alternative to the influence of Profitism's expectations, challenges, motivations, greed, absence of support systems, and punishment of those unsuccessful in the system. If you can think of any other even possible explanation, let me know.

If we wish to 'treat' this malady, we must go way beyond increasing taxes on booze, beyond fiddling around with opening and closing hours, beyond policing the booze providers for serving the drunk, beyond ticking off the parents for their 'lack of control' over their children. Nothing less than a complete societal shakeup can dent this symptom of societal disintegration.

Hopeless hopelessness

The alienated young, together with the homeless and the underclass generally, are not only without hope, they are in a state of hopeless hopelessness. That is, they cannot even hope to be hopeful. This condition is the wretched child of powerlessness, lack of influence other than via withdrawal, or by violent and Q3 acts against any and all aspects of the society from which they feel they have been locked out. Michael Connelly, in <u>Concrete Blond</u>, notes that his main character, Hieronymus Bosch, knew that "...hope was the lifeblood of the heart. Without it there was nothing, only darkness." Drunk is dark.

Gangs of alienated youth come about when the young don't feel connected to the broader society. To 'have not' does not refer simply to a lack of money and all it can buy, but to lack of experiences, specifically, to absence of Q1 experiences. R D Laing (*Politics of Experience*, p24), writes, "Our behaviour is a function of our experience. We act according to the way we see things. *If our experience is destroyed our behaviour will be destructive.*" [my italics]

By experience, particularly in childhood, Laing is referring to positive experiences of love itself, of safety in home and food provision, stimulation and support, of sharing and co-operation and community, of encouragement to search, experiment, create. How old fashioned that Q1 catalogue sounds. Not exactly the global Profitist ethic, expectation or requirement.

The extreme and the average

I have demonstrated that much of our experience has deteriorated over the past 50 years. We can see the direction of things more clearly if we take a look at extreme examples of the trends.

Two 16 year old girls in Perth had for some time been asking themselves and each other what it would feel like to kill someone. Because she was handy they strangled a 15 year old girlfriend. One said later "As our friend, we did not really want her to suffer". "We just did it because we felt like it, it is hard to explain," the other girl said. "I knew we had wanted to kill someone before. We knew it was wrong, but it didn't feel wrong at all, it just felt right."

A couple of years ago in Melbourne an unfortunate man came across two 16 year old girls hanging from the same branch of a tree. Both had been addicts of MySpace.com, and both had written there in praise of suicide. Their final entry was: "RIP Jodie & Steph".

Reactions and responses

Two partnerships of two girls, the behaviour of each wildly outside what most of us would consider 'normal limits'. Watch the incidence of such events, previously next to unknown, increase. If we are not to attribute the responsibility for such outrages against humanity to the Profitist zeitgeist, to what may we attribute it? Weak parental control? Poorly trained and motivated teachers? Mercury in retrograde? To me the most chilling aspect of all such terrible events is that the powers that be, political, commercial, religious, educational, medical, psychological, tut tut and move on. As a society we experience no urgency about such matters, have no concern to try to get to the bottom of them. Why not? Because our consciousness and conscience have been anaesthetised and are therefore dormant. Why do the churches rave on about abortion and ignore adolescent murder and suicide? Why are all our priorities so hopelessly out of whack?

Neither of the girl death-dealing double acts was a front page splash in Australia's main newspapers. I can tell you, with absolute certainty, that in the 1950s either event would have covered Australian front pages for a week. I recall a rape in Perth, Western Australia, and it covered the front pages of the local papers. Now, a rape or a run of the mill murder is so ho hum it's lucky if it rates a mention anywhere in the news sections of a newspaper, let alone be headlined. We are just so used to, so anaesthetized by repetition of, such extreme examples of bestiality that we have become dulled to how simply *unacceptable* they are in a civilised society. Muslims claim current Western societies are not civilised. Clearly, they are right, and don't remind me of unacceptable practices in societies under Muslim control. What they do is their business. What we do is ours.

The cone of distraction

A pervasive phenomenon that bothers me is the extent to which the young have built firewalls around themselves. Most noticeably, they live a life of surround sound, keeping the immediate environment and any intrusive thoughts at arms length with Ipod, mobile phone, and now the iPhone and its clones. When was the last time you saw a young person, walking or in public transport, observing and enjoying the passing parade? When outdoors in park or forest they need ghetto blasters or ear phones to keep the water, trees and birds at bay. I hate to see music used to force unhappy thoughts and realisations – their bleak reality – from intruding into consciousness. Ipods in particular are used to cocoon the mind. They don't want to hear the world around them. This denies them the opportunity to think, and helps them to maintain ignorance and to stay with the familiar. It ensures that they don't have to, in fact cannot, think or reflect at all.

The ubiquitous phone

Almost every young person on a bus or train clacks away on their phone, maintaining contact with their friends from whom they cannot be out of touch for five minutes. They are alienated from all others. If they find themselves with time to think they will be forced to confront all the unnatural forces arraigned against them – absence of an, absence of informed or relevant guidance from their parents, the emptiness of booze and drugs, the unlikelihood of rewarding and rewarded work, the almost certain eventual breakdown of extended relationships, including marriage, the certainty they will be pushed around in the service of the global man, the spiritual emptiness of their lives. They want to shut down their brains and keep them shut. Computer games and net surfing serve the same purpose, as do rave dance parties, with thousands of floppy dolls bouncing up and down as the Ecstasy travels their veins and scrambles their brains.

Are they like 'us'?

The young today do *not* behave as my generation behaved. All oldies claim things aren't what they used to be, by which they mean, things are getting worse fast. On the positive side, and compared with at least my generation, today's young mature much earlier, and one-on-one and in small groups in a formal setting are as thoughtful and delightful as we think we were. More so. I am tremendously impressed with Generations X and Y, and expect to be with Gen Z,but only face to face and where they are deliberately engaged in life affirming activities.

There is a negative side, as though all the young have been born under the sign of Gemini. Today's youth are more creative than were we in our day, producing fascinating music, visual arts, writing, digital productivity of all kinds. Then off they go and suicide or wipe themselves out with booze and drugs, or at best take a lousy job because only work output with perceived commercial value is recruited and rewarded. They drink much more alcohol than we did at their age, have sex way before we did, and take drugs we would have been reluctant to approach.

And, as noted earlier, they use music and mobile phones to protect themselves from awareness of their vulnerable and therefore frightening situation. The radio stations they listen to seem to recognise this need to avoid thinking time: as one track is about to end they run over it with the beginning of the next – no break (silence) permitted. Likewise they rarely back-announce tracks because to do so would leave a tiny window for reflection. And the program presenters compound this by talking and giggling very fast without end.

Consideration

The negative side is nowhere more obvious than when the young are out and about. In the street or in crowded public transport, they turn into selfish, thoughtless, rude, cold little buggers. Where have consideration, courtesy, thoughtfulness, gone? What do these words mean to the young I wonder? Why do they seem so free from them most of the time? They show every sign of possessing these Q1 qualities when the circumstances are right, e.g., helping out at tsunami time, saving someone from the surf or fire, yet lack it in their everyday life. It is almost invariably the young who:

bump old people out of the way,

rarely offer their seat to the needy,

use their shopping trolley to cut across you in the supermarket,

stroll across intersections to interfere with turning cars – they are invincible and oncoming cars do not exist, or cross the road without a glance either way,

treat teachers with open contempt,

thoughtfully drop their empty Maccas containers and drink bottles over your fence (they could have put them in your letter box,)

talk loudly on their mobile phones, seeming to be unaware of the personal spaces of people near them,

in crowded public transport, spread themselves and their belongings over three times the room they need, and then wear an almost comical expression of rebellion or assumed indifference,

cut into the traffic, seemingly, again, unaware of any inconvenience caused, and

ditto make a three point turn anywhere in a street, rather than turn into a driveway and wait their turn to rejoin the traffic…

…and so on ad infinitum.

Message

What do each of these examples, and any number of similar occurrences, tell us about what the young person is *automatically* feeling or thinking at the time of the 'offence'? Each is an instance of indifference towards others, coupled with a determination to 'win' in some totally insignificant-seeming situation. Each is directed against a person unknown to the offender – there is nothing personal in any of this.

The message in every case is very clear: they are saying,

FUCK YOU!

Not *felt* with any particular hostility, just automatic ... you, in my way, my life is shit anyway, this is for *me*.

This is an unconscious backlash

Now why are they saying that, with every show of cold indifference or surly determination? [Don't remind me of exceptions: I am talking about worrying and clear trends.] How and why are the young so split in their personality? How can they reconcile their true maturity, sweetness, insight, compassion when put to the test, with their bloody-mindedness in so many of their dealings with the rest of the world? They're fine with each other, but are seriously unattractive in their automatic and discourteous response to other non-young people and to all and everything which seems to them to be competing for the good things, no matter how trifling. Not wealth and possessions, but the seat on the bus, the position in the line, the surrounding personal spaces, the position in the line of cars, in fact anything that makes them feel potentially *diminished* or *misused*. They feel they are constantly in *competition* for minor, trivial gains and advantages.

Is this deliberate on their part? Sometimes yes, as seen in the sourly gleeful expression produced by some insignificant triumph of convenience. Mostly, this endless, take no prisoners, show no mercy, battle against 'them' is, I am sure, unconscious. Way out of all proportion to the actual gains achieved. They do not have it in them to *consider* others, to acknowledge them as equally human with equally legitimate needs. This is what Profitism has reduced them to. If you don't win you don't come second or third, you *lose*. If you are not beautiful you are ugly and must do something expensive about it. You will work for the man until you drop. Deep down, and not all that deep, they *know* they are being manipulated, are being ripped off at every turn. They must lash back somehow. The Profitists are beyond their reach, and are in any case wonderfully protected by propaganda and their PR machines. There are only 'other people' to take the brunt of their alienation.

I am so grateful I am not young, seeking direction in life and a fair opportunity. Many young people will deny my bleak picture, but I would not be young now for all the blessings of Profitism.

A metaphor of sorts

The brain is not limitless in its capacity to create mind and memory. As we get older something starts to fizzle out, and there is a controversy among scientists as to whether brain cells die or connections wither, or both. In either case, as we get older we progressively forget bits of the past, names, events, etc., then where things are and where to put things, then people we used to recognize, then how things are used, what they are for, and so on. These latter are examples of dementia.

I have forgotten a great deal, all or most of it trivial stuff such as names of actors past, books I have read, even recently, unless I read them again and think, this sounds familiar. In other words, I am progressively losing *what I don't need*. This is inconvenient or embarrassing but unimportant. So far I have been left with my thinking and creating apparatus untouched. I fully anticipate the time when this will no longer be the case.

By whatever magic, yet to be unravelled by science, the mind rearranges itself so we manage to get by with less and less capacity. The brain can handle only so much.

An evil parallel

Profitism generally and New Profitism in particular are working on the brain in an analogous manner. They take the healthy collective brain of the citizenry, especially of the young, and overload it, overstuff it with unavoidable material which squeezes out what is not needed in, is irrelevant to, a Profitist society. Quite aside from the incompatibility of Human Values and the Profit Motive, Profitism is ensuring there is *no room* for both.

By stuffing us with the unyielding, unrestrained, 24/7 onslaught in praise of me, me, me and buy, buy, buy and win, win, win, New Profitism in particular is squeezing out concepts, motives and desires relating to Human Values, all the Q1 values of compassion, generosity, moral courage and the rest. These get no air time because *nobody thinks of them*. And nobody thinks of them because those thoughts, qualities and concepts *have been replaced*. As the cuckoo chick pushes all the legitimate chicks out of the nest and consumes everything the frantic parents can provide, so New Profitism has us feeding and nourishing it with our money, our desires, our fears, and we remain only vaguely aware that it is the only winner and cares only for itself. And *that* is why tension, alienation, violence, unhappiness and hopelessness abound. We have lost touch with our true selves.

Concerns and desires which once played a *part* in every girl's teenage life, now fill her awareness of life to overflowing. There is no room for both sets of competing concerns, those to do with Human Values, and those focussed on me, me, me. To some extent the boys are being sucked in too (new Brut deodorant is still brutally male, here is the latest range of expensive designer clothes that you, yes you young man, must wear to the Melbourne cup), but although they are just as self absorbed as the girls they are much more selfish, which keeps their thinking processes closer to historical precedents, sport, mind changing substances and sex, sex, sex. These preoccupations keep them better immunised against mind-content replacement. But watch: someone will think of a way to do it, maybe through virtual sex on the web, yeah, that'd work.

The reason the young have constructed their own world online is that they want to cut themselves off from everybody else – via YouTube, MySpace, Facebook, Bebo, Twitterk, mobile phone addiction – and operate as a giant billion-component cell, a vast tribe, outside the appalling remainder of society. We are not in touch with them, nor they with us. How's that for alienation?

Gavin Sinclair

10 THE OLD AND THE UNEMPLOYABLE

One of our society's greatest denials of reality, or refusal to accept what is, occurs around advancing age and the changes it brings. Why on earth are we so petrified of getting or looking older? What is it that encourages, virtually enforces a view of age as repugnant, and that we must do everything in our power to slow and preferably halt its advance, or _reverse_ it? What else but Profitism, as represented in this case by the 'beauty' industry, which makes the appearance of cellulite seem a visitation of evil, or a wrinkle a sign of genuine disintegration of personal integrity? Ageing and signs of ageing are revolting, and must be expensively dealt with, as outlined _ad nauseum_ by the joined-at-the-hip supporters of New Profitism - girls' and women's magazines and TV commercials.

Only in Western societies are older people ignored or held in contempt. Only in Western societies is it believed that youth has the answer to all difficulties and conundrums. Those who know least rule, OK? Profitism does not _need_ knowledge and wisdom: it needs energy, aggression, competitiveness and greed. In most societies the old are still treasured and revered for their experience and their advice, that is, advice on how to live and love. This is of no use to Profitism. Beyond a certain age people become nothing but a brake, a burden.

Get thee behind me, or at least out of sight

Consider the nursing home and, to a lesser extent, the retirement village. There is no originality in condemning such institutions as Q3 masquerading as Q1 and Q2. In even the best run and inmate-focused nursing homes, only the dedication of overworked staff and visiting entertainers are or can be Q1. Such institutions have arisen, of course, as a consequence of the demise of the extended family, coupled with the need for double incomes. For some time now the younger generations have been unable to look after the elderly. Progressively there has been neither room nor time for the previous generation.

The ridiculous pressures of modern living force young families to attend only to the most pressing of their immediate needs. The most honest among us acknowledge that getting the oldies off our hands is not entirely without its benefits. So the elderly are deposited in farewell dumping grounds.

The waiting game

Retirement villages are little better than nursing homes, representing a gathering place, an oasis, for those who have effectively lost real and enjoyable contact with children and other younger relatives, and seek each other for an alternative form of comfort. Not quite farewell yet, but the clock ticks.

For so long as profit remains the primary focus of the society, this situation cannot change. Depositories for the aged are profitable and we have been persuaded there is no alternative. I will totter out to sea before I submit to retirement village or nursing home.

Gavin Sinclair

A delve into speculative fiction

It is clear that in many societies there will be an ever-expanding number of elderly and old. Many well meaning people are already wondering how these groups are to be supported. Recent statistics suggest that in Australia at present there are about five people in employment for each person aged 65 and over. The projection is for that number to drop to less than three workers per 65+ person by 2050. How can so few incomes, producing such reduced income tax, support such large numbers?

Yes it's a problem, but it is not the only one, or possibly even the main one. Here are some projections, which I would convert into a novel if I had the skills:

Already, unskilled and semi-skilled workers are finding it difficult to find work.

The trend away from employing humans to do work which can be done better and cheaper by machines will continue and accelerate.

The machines will increasingly be robotised, and will eventually become fully autonomous robots.

This trend will increase the already present stressful demand for everyone to study for and attain qualifications of some sort. The days of leaving school at 14 or 15 and expecting a fruitful working life are going, going, gone.

Eventually, all mining and transport activities will be done by robots and machines, controlled by humans.

Then the robots will become intelligent enough to respond to the environment themselves, and make their own decisions, thereby eliminating the clever jobs that were controlling them.

And employment? Already those being laid off say they 'don't know anything but mining', or truck driving, or telling money in a bank. What will they be able to retrain for?

The unemployables will be able to find work only as low paid 'usefuls', to use the ugly mining industry work category, or as serfs or as slaves.

The emphasis on a qualification as essential will be fine or at least OK for those who can benefit from such studies.

But what of the at least 15% of citizens who do not have the intellectual wherewithal to tackle any course of study successfully?

Will they have to be supported, along with the old? In a Profitist society? You must be joking.

As robots and machines replace most human work, the unemployable proportion of the population must increase until it is a majority. They will have nothing to do, a recipe for . . . .

Please come up with an appropriate ending to the book.

And, while you're at it, to the human race.

Where's the hole in that argument, that temporal progression?

Young = market for us, Old = useless, a burden

To Profitism the young, the pre-contributing young, are nothing but, *nothing but*, a market begging for exploitation. They are hopelessly naïve, pathetically suggestible, mindless slaves to fashion and peer group pressure. All you have to do is propagandize the fashions that suit Profitism and you're in like Flynn.

As to the old, well, gimme a break. What can they contribute except experience, common sense, a hard earned morality, even wisdom if you dig for it? What can they contribute? Buggerall! Youth is King and Queen. We have told them so and made sure they believe it.

Ah, things are going well. Look at the balance sheet. Wow.

Profitism and the Family

Approximate timing	Profitism-serving transition
To 1919	For the well off, extended families
	For the poor, large broods
1920s to the depression	Profitism-fueled self indulgence starts to fracture families
1930s to end of WW2	Profitism-caused depression accelerates family disintegration, exacerbated by WW2 upheavel
Post-war, 1945-1960s	Enter the nuclear family, two parents, 2 - 3 kids. Profitism's salvation. Consumerism takes off in a big way, until the 1960s shake the nuclear family foundations
1970s to, say, 2020	The (so far) hay day of New Profitism. Traditional 'nuclear family' gone. 25% of homes now single-occupied. No more community. We can hope things start to turn around from here.

Gavin Sinclair

11 HOW NEW PROFITISM WORKS

Chapters 6 and 7 outlined a large number of instances of the more or less direct impact the unbridled Profit Motive has on the Western world and its citizens. The key entry in those chapters was the final question, why do we stand for it? By now it must be clear that for so long as Profitism holds sway most people will never have the experience of God within, will never experience the Q1 qualities they desire. You may see my attack on Profitism as irrelevant to spiritual growth. In <u>Become happy</u>... the reader was introduced to some steps that could be taken to experience God in yourself and in your life, and it's perfectly reasonable if you wish to focus entirely on yourself and ignore the wider picture.

The Profitist ethic, an oxymoron if ever there was one, has so thoroughly flooded the world and the minds of the populations that it's primacy seems as natural and unremarkable as water flowing downhill instead of up. We just don't notice it. We take it for granted, much as mothers in some societies assume that only a proportion of their children will survive childhood. The task I have set myself is to wake people up to Profitism's true nature and effects.

How can we account for all the wretchedness and unhappiness we see around us? If it is not down to Profitism, then what? We can't blame communism. Terrorism is distracting, but is so recent a significant phenomenon that it cannot possibly be held responsible for our chaotic and, for far too many, desperate circumstances. If Profitism had cared, the third world would be without poverty, hunger and disease *now*.

Can we at least agree that a good case can be made that Profitism is responsible for our societies' disintegration? Let's look at the mechanisms underlying Profitism's takeover of the Western world's consciousness and learn how this was achieved. These mechanisms and the transitions which have flowed from them are presented here in no particular order. They are so many and various they are impossible to categorize, but I want you to get a *feeling* for how ubiquitous and all-consuming has the Profitist ethic become.

Lies and bullshit

The main reason Profitism, with supporters and apologists, has been so successful is because the entire system has mastered the art of persuasion. They have achieved this by pouring billions of dollars and working days into designing, developing and using ever more sophisticated marketing and advertising techniques, to the point where these have become truer than truth. My fellow psychologists, to their shame, have played a leading role in this mind management of the masses.

Life is not full of belly laughs. One of the best I ever experienced (you had to be there) was via a sketch in Rowan and Martin's Laugh-in – pretty girl on screen with cute upturning side plaits as chords from well known song from Oklahoma build introduction, and she flashes the teeth and sings jauntily: "Ah'm jes' a gal who cain't say n-n-n." Struggles harder. "N-n-nyich …. N-N-N-n-nyah". Nope, can't do it.

That's how I am with bullshit. I speak truth, as I understand it, as often as I can. Otherwise I lie. But I doubt you'll ever catch me bullshitting. I am indebted for the clear distinction I now see between lies and bullshit to an American philosopher, Harry Frankfurt. Go to...

http://www.gwinnettdailyonline.com/articleB5BD6D4417 AF444DBD8F9770AA729B26.asp

The article is written in philosophese, and can be heavy going, but absolutely nails what lying is, what bullshitting is, how to tell one from the other and which is the more destructive of truth. Liars know what is true and deliberately speak to convince others that something else is true which they know is not. The bullshitter has no interest in the truth of a situation, either to speak for the truth or to oppose it. What is important is to give the impression that you know what you're talking about. This is at the core, for example, of all TV commercials. This is also the core talent required by those who join debating societies – the skill to dazzle with sophistry ('A plausible but misleading or fallacious argument'. Answers.com. Our former Prime Minister, John Howard, once a champion debater, is a Master of the Art).

Most effective politicians in Australia are as good at lying as they are at bullshitting. A famous lie was the assertion that would-be refugees callously threw their children overboard in order to save themselves, a statement repeated many times and known to be a lie. Alternatively, here is some bullshit: "No government has done more for the welfare of the Australian people than this government." The thing about bullshit is that it does not matter whether or not it is true. What matters is that people believe it to be true, i.e., that it be believable, credible and, in the political and commercial context, whether people gain a favourable impression of the bullshitter.

Yours fatally, Profitism

Advertising material and public relations statements are rarely caught out in a lie because they don't have to lie. Lies are too easily identified. Bullshit can never be caught out because it makes no assertions that could be put to any truth test. The relevant truth need not be important. I mean, who cares which shampoo adds more shine? Bullshitters must keep away even from consideration of truth or they could not sleep at night. The public, under the constant and overwhelming barrage of the 360 degree bullshit attack, has become progressively unable to judge truth, and is encouraged to care even less.

Sometimes truth squeezes through, as now with global warming. When irresistible evidence piles up in favour of a truth, to the point where the contrary lies are caught out, only the bullshit remains. Most politicians are skilled at shifting from lies to bullshit – yes, it does seem that the climate is changing, but the effects are being greatly exaggerated by the leftist chardonnay-sippers. "Greatly exaggerated" is perfect bullshit, being challengeable only in weasel words as vague as itself.

Telling truth and telling lies have one thing in common: they are both focused on the truth, one to promote it, the other to oppose it while knowing it to be true. At least, truth is the issue. As Frankfurt has it, "[The liar] must design his false-hood under the guidance of that truth." Bullshit is truth-irrelevant, and therefore "...bullshit is a greater enemy of the truth than lies are." You and I, every day, are saturated, marinated, in bullshit. Those of us old enough to remember a more truth-telling time can see this. The young cannot.

Persuasion

Joseph Goebbels knew only too well, having updated the technique, that a lie stated often enough becomes true for the target audience. Humanist Clive Hamilton put it very well: "When deploying the big-lie technique there are rules to be followed; be audacious; never admit fault; never accept the possibility of alternatives; and repeat the falsehood so often that people end up accepting it as truth." [Sydney Morning Herald, 9 May 2007] Considered one by one, the Profitist lies are not up there with 'all Jews are evil and secretly control the world', but collectively their influence has been profound.

There are still, out there somewhere, people trying hard to undo some anti Human Values Profitist outrage, but the propaganda onslaught from all media quarters ensures that their views are on and stay on starvation rations. We are all aware of the vast array of things we feel are not as they should be, but we have somehow been conned into believing that they could not be much different. The poor are always with us, etc. We have been bludgeoned into feeling that these occurrences just happen, are simply part of the rich (or poor, as the case may be) tapestry of life. Communism was the only part way successful opponent of Profitism: part successful because it controlled the lives of so many people for quite a long time, but in the end a total failure in the ways already discussed.

And while all this is developing and engulfing us, where is God? Nothing happens but that God allows it (Muktananda). As a Guru rarely intrudes into a devotee's karma (nor into their own for that matter) by, say, curing them of a fatal disease, so God is not going to 'save us' until we wake up to ourselves and do something for him to support.

God is waiting for us to open our eyes and act.

Yours fatally, Profitism

Lost for words

PRSpeak, promotion, marketing, advertising and spin doctoring have corrupted and bastardised useful words. 'Amazing' is attached to things which are, at best, mildly diverting. Similarly with icon, legend, chaos, breathtaking, awesome, tragedy, outraged, disaster, delicious, perfect. This weakening of our strong descriptors makes a reference to anything truly outstanding or unique sound like a TV commercial, and therefore basically phoney.

Awesome is a good example. There was a time when to be in awe of a person or experience meant something. Students at Oxford were in awe of their Dons, Irish peasants were in awe of their priests, and so on. If you watched a volcano erupt you could definitely use the word awesome as a descriptor. Now, however, it is also awesome to be able to buy three Cokes for the price of two. You can watch every ball of the test cricket on your 3G mobile for only five dollars a month; now I call that awesome! The word's meaning is down from a banquet to a bun. In the shadow of George Orwell I assert that soon we will not be able to describe anything of beauty, magnitude, importance or value adequately. Such words have been hijacked by and are being dissolved in mercenaric acid.

Whatever happened to generosity?

Take another and more important example. Generosity is losing its meaning. If you give *in order* to receive, you kill the experience of generosity by the giver and of gratitude by the receiver. Acts of true generosity have just about disappeared. Most foreign aid, given by rich to poor nations, comes with strings attached, usually to do with favourable trade or political influence. At a more local level gifts and benefits are passed around for a return favour, or at least with the donor's name revealed so the generosity can come to public notice. The spin doctors deprive the apparently good act of any virtue. The act of seeming generosity has become as cold blooded as a company's price rise or mass sacking. Profitism has completely churned useful words and their meanings to its own advantage.

Just as an aside, and oddly, they have left some words alone. Magnificent is an example. Just going down MSWord's thesaurus, add superb, wonderful, glorious (excepting hair shine), brilliant (ditto), superlative. I guess they're just waiting their turn to be bastardised.

A final example, decent, decency. This has not been corrupted, it has been obliterated. We used to say, he's a decent sort of a bloke, or, at least have the decency to apologise to her for what you said. That is, call on your conscience and act accordingly. This is the concept that is disappearing, taking words like upright, honest, sincere, with it.

Profit *über alles*

Muslims have a case when they assert that Profitist behaviour - exploitation, profiteering and hypocrisy - is sinful. They have in mind the *big* exploiters, the globals, not the many examples of relatively true free enterprise, the smaller companies not seeking a global reach. The globals are aided and abetted by the governments of the lands in which they operate, which support their intellectual, commercial and social plunder of target markets. China is the most recent example of transition from a mixture of a controlled industrial and peasant economy, to one in which Western corporations are invited to come in and access a giant market and cheap, desperate labour force. The only proviso is that the Chinese themselves, and particularly the Chinese government, can get in for a major whack of the goodies.

India is following down, and I mean down, the same track. In developing nations, including China and India, the market-driven, profit-driven economy is now accepted as holy writ, soon to lead to the pluses and minuses with which we in the west have become familiar. In non-Western Profitist and quasi-Profitist societies, many people starve to death and are left to expire in miserable monochrome. In Western societies few starve to death or even go close. And there is colourful commercial television. Bread and circuses never did a better job. Surely, you may cry, this is better than ignorance and starvation? Yes it is, but can we do no better?

Speaking of jobs

We can distinguish between jobs which add direct value to the lives of people, jobs which serve Profitism, and jobs which keep everything grinding on.

Among the first group are doctors, nurses, paramedics, ambulance drivers, counsellors, primary, secondary and tertiary teachers, garbos, cleaners, firemen, carers, church workers: continue this list to your own satisfaction. Some well paid, the vast bulk poorly paid. Nurses and teachers, for example, are forced to work for below average wages because their work is, as the powerful repeatedly tell them as though they need to hear it, so intrinsically rewarding. Such humbug and hypocrisy. The intrinsic nature of this Q1 benefit is the *only* high value reward in such work. Those with the purse strings use it against such workers, underpaying them for the 'privilege' of doing Human Values work.

The second group comprises jobs that serve Profitism, and exist to serve and enrich the shareholders. Our societies are structured so most people have to 'go to work' to 'earn a living'. Such telling phrases. Go to work, because we are moved around and domiciled where Profitists choose. Look at the vast concrete termite mounds rising in Beijing to house the slum dwellers of the future, but hey, they're close to work. The Chinese have learned a thing or two from the West. One of my early radicalising experiences occurred in 1956 in Stoke-on-Trent, as I was hitching from London to Liverpool. I was up early ready, to seek my next hitch, and heard a loud whistle blow. Instantly, as though for a movie director, scores of identical seeming men poured out of a string of grimy little terraces, crossed the road and disappeared into a large, equally grimy pottery opposite. Within moments they had all disappeared. I knew then that nobody should have to live and work like that if there was any alternative available. Of course, there was none.

The third group of jobs, jobs that keep everything grinding on, can be found in public bureaucracies, each of which must answer to a politician, federal, state or local. Why are such bureaucracies so awful to deal with? Why are so many of the employees so dull, dead, lazy-seeming (most are not lazy; they are overworked these days), moving in slomo, mixed in with preposterous forms and other paper work requiring hours for completion and bearing only slight relevance to the enquiry or enquirer?

It is widely acknowledged that senior bureaucrats once had the system-supported confidence to advise politicians independently and frankly, whether or not it was likely the advice would be well received.

This is no longer the case. In a significant change from the past, publicly funded bureaucracies, as distinct from bureaucracies which keep Profitist enterprises clicking along, promote people who are docile and compliant. These promotions often occur in response to pressure from political masters, who themselves wish to serve Profitism or to enlarge their sphere of influence. When the politicians are replaced by a change of government, so now are the senior bureaucrats also replaced. The newcomers are chosen for their willingness to love, cherish and obey *their* master. Each new minister wants their *own* boy or girl in charge. Any show of independence is crushed: Sydney Ferries has had 11 CEOs in the past 15 years. NSW State Rail has had nine in the past ten. What has fed this trend?

Terror at the top produces indecisiveness and cowardice among lower-level employees, the cowardice resulting from having done something which upset someone higher up, who then exploded all over the place at the victim's expense, and entered on the employee's personnel file, "too independent", "cannot be relied on". "not to be re-employed in the public service." Extreme caution and covert lack of commitment come to replace any sense of pitching in and doing something you think is right in the circumstances. Thus are decisions deferred and referred upwards and sideways, with everyone ducking and weaving to avoid any clear responsibility for the action or suggestion. This also explains the plethora of meetings. If everyone talks about something a hundred times, any eventual outcome, if unsuccessful, cannot be sheeted home to anyone in particular. For all who might otherwise like to do a useful job this is disheartening, dispiriting, demoralising, and goes some way towards explaining the mood state apparent in most large bureaucracies.

Gavin Sinclair

Service industry boom

In Australia there are two main growth areas in the economy: mineral resources, especially iron ore and coal, and tourism with all its offshoots, hospitality, bar work, etc. Another industry, telemarketing and telesurveying, was booming but is shrinking again as such jobs are chasing tens of thousands of manufacturing jobs overseas, to India and South East Asia.

Governments, with eyes on the unemployment figures, must be delighted with the increase in the number of service jobs, jobs in which an individual is underpaid to provide a service to corporations or companies, or to people who have real jobs. If you're prepared to stretch the definition a little, most jobs fall into this broad category of 'service'. In corporations and companies, and occasionally in the public service, senior jobs can be real jobs; they allow, to some extent, for exercise of authority or imagination or intellect.

But below a certain point lies the vast majority of jobs and these are all service jobs in the sense that they are performed as a rather mindless and unsatisfying service to those with jobs higher up in the chain of service to shareholders. Until recently blue collar jobs carried a degree of work satisfaction. This is changing, as the efficiency experts require ever faster work turnover, with reduced concern for work quality. Shades of the early 1900s. How come we have allowed the exponential growth in futureless jobs to occur and to diminish the natural enthusiasm and optimism of the young? We are letting them down badly.

Progress and development

When I was young, the Profitist cry in support of their activities was 'You can't stop progress.' This was chanted against anybody who questioned the destruction or conversion of the environment for profit, or similar attacks upon buildings and areas deserving conservation. Now, of course, the cliché of choice is 'development'. Such a positive, cheery term, implying that something that was backward, inferior, past its prime, is about to be transformed into something better, exciting and cool. Nobody, certainly not the media, seems to notice that all 'development' was and is to the benefit of the already wealthy and well off. And the developers operate seamlessly through the political parties and politicians they have influenced or purchased in advance. Everyone knows it. Nobody cares. We are too far gone in cynicism and helplessness. Where have you seen a 'development' for the common man and woman? Well stap mah mouth! Don't I just sound like a whingeing old lefty, steeped in envy for the treasures of the deserving? As so often before, why is it so?

Why did subtlety have to go?

We are living in a gross world, a world without subtlety in any significant area of activity: politics, business, industry and commerce, art, education, entertainment. Exemplifying this is modern art, so chaotic, so grungy, and so riddled with pretension, emptiness and brevity.

This nastiness is accompanied by the death of romance. Compare the Beatles' *I wanna hold your hand* with Steve Miller's recent *Abracadabra*:

1   2   3   4   1   2   3   4   1   2   3   4

Ab   RA   c'   DABra

1   2   3   4 1   2   3   4   1

I wanna REACHOU tn   GRABya

In movies today, romance cannot live in company with rape and violence. In earlier times it could: it was the juxtaposition of death and violence with love and romance that underpinned so many of the great tragedies. Today, love and romance have been sequestered into vacuous romcoms and coming of age titillations.

Wander around any video/dvd rental establishment and compare the number of love stories with the number of horror / violence / sadism / brutality offerings. You will come up with a rather spooky figure. In these movies nothing can be suggested or implied, everything must be shown full frontal. People are no longer shot and fall over. They must be exploded, with bits of body, blood and gore everywhere, superseded by more of the same to the accompaniment of a 110db sound track. Market research must be telling the marketers this is what people want. Why?

Why easier?

Why does everything have to get simpler, easier, to require less effort? Anything that really does take drudgery out of work is to be accepted with gratitude – washing machines, the internal combustion engine, computers with adequate speed and power, etc. Similarly, we can welcome many things that replace less useful devices – the refrigerator replacing the ice chest, the car replacing the horse, word processing replacing the typewriter, etc. The

Profitist ethic as it has become insists that everything, every little aspect of everything, should follow this trend – from unlocked car (1900s), to car locked requiring a key to open the door (1920s+), to remote unlocking by pressing a button to save us from having to turn a key through 45 degrees (1970s?), to keyless entry (1990s?). Next will come voice recognition door opening (2010s), closely followed by hardware and software for authorised brainwave recognition (2020s?).

That is to open a car door, but think how much money all the developers, manufacturers, warehousers, marketers, advertisers and retailers make from such constant 'improvements'. Multiply this development by all the thousands of things we use – the toothpaste cap the top of which lifts to save us from the effort of unscrewing it – and you have a consumer society going on forever, or until all raw materials are exhausted, which will be never as recycling of everything will be a major industry of the future. Nearly all of these 'advances' is Q3, with a small minority being Q2, as in, for example, ever faster cars. Again, the societal direction is away from Q1 and towards the world of Q3.

Why now?

The Profit Motive needs and therefore encourages focus on the instant. Nothing should be bought on lay-by. The article must be bought now, used now, found disappointing very soon (without prior notification the new improved version becomes available next week much to your annoyance), replaced as soon as marketing can persuade people of the inferiority of the perfectly satisfactory thing they bought. This is not planned obsolescence, as many high tech products are very well made: it is simply marketing-based planned *replacement*.

The marketing techniques will make us want and buy the later version. Against this are no countervailing education, advice or pressure.

This barrage of 'you must buy now' is one reason the young, in fact all but the old, demand that they experience everything now. Another key contributor is television's short-grab-focussed compulsion, which engenders the short time span. We are all, of course, bombarded with propaganda persuading us that we deserve nothing less, and as soon as some succumb, peer pressure and envy bring in the rest. This means that young people today never experience the thrill of barely bearable expectation, nor the joy and satisfaction of eventual fulfilment. They are not aware of it, but the absence of these from their experience is a sad omission. If we run our lives so that as soon as a desire is felt its realisation is only hours away, we will reach a point where there seems to be nothing out there which will or can provide satisfaction, joy, accomplishment. Because everything is acquired via credit card debt, nothing is paid for as part of the act of acquisition. Sure you pay later, but at the time of 'purchase' you are getting it for nothing. There is no sense of having earned it. It is just something I need now, so the pleasure of anticipation is absent and the thrill of acquisition fades quickly.

Chucking out the past

When I was young I was contemptuous of society's long time institutions, norms and practices, particularly marriage, christenings, and taking formal leave of the dead. In my ignorance I was unaware that these practices serve fundamental human needs for recognition of categorical status and for an end point. In some societies marriage occurs to prove that a man owns one or more women. In Western societies it is a public promise of commitment, of loyalty to each other, with those getting married feeling strongly that they will not be joining the divorce lines any time soon. Now the ethos is having a good time: who needs ritual or connections to the past? Profitism has schooled us to want only stimulation and pleasure, but we do need our institutions. They are archetypes built deep within us all. We toss them out at our peril.

Places and modes of worship

To recognise how far the Churches have taken us from the God experience is not to ignore or to deny them their proper role, which was excellently outlined by Kevin Rudd, then shadow Minister for External Affairs: "The function of the church in all … areas of social, economic and security policy is to speak directly to the state: to give power to the powerless, voice to those who have none, and to point to the great silences in our national discourse where otherwise there are no natural advocates." [The Monthly, Oct '06, p26] Now that he is Prime Minister, it will be instructive to see whether he encourages and practises what he preaches.

The main churches keep people from experiencing God by ignoring the truly terrible things people do to each other, either as individuals or as directors of armaments and armies, while focussing on and fiercely denouncing what people do for pleasure in cooperation with others. Most sermons are simply exhortations for people to do what they cannot do – reverse their own natures and limitations. Such preachy waffling might be nice but is pointless without practical guidance on how to achieve the lofty aims.

Profitism's excesses are coming to be accepted as a law of nature, acceptable because they must be accepted. The Church has therefore shrunken its view of moral and immoral behaviour to the point where it can't see beyond the continuing relaxation of sexual mores. God is present only in the clichés and platitudes.

The ersatz choice

One of the major lies put about by Profitists and right wing politicians is that their activities are directed towards providing the population with more choice. This is claimed for the vast range of consumer goods, and also by politicians trying to persuade us that forcing us to choose right now between two undesirable processes is preferable to being given genuine information which would allow us to make a rational decision. Everywhere the phoney choice is on the rise and the genuine choice is disappearing.

The shrinkage of real choice, for me personally the death of fresh Moore's bread and the disappearance of Griffin's Ginger Nuts, is not a serious matter. As a trend it is serious. Supermarkets increasingly drop off items which do not pass the turnover test. This will eventually reduce real choice to the lowest common denominator: another of the four hundred blows aimed at reducing and eventually eliminating discernment, the ability to distinguish quality from crap. Quality always sells in smaller numbers because it is more expensive, is uneconomical, is dead soon, OK? What we must have is turnover.

And the choices we are left with? Let's stay with supermarkets. Dozens of breads, scores of toothpastes and brushes, hundreds of shampoos, deodorants, pads for that time of the month, uncountable (add pharmacies) skin preparations – thousands of choices to solve a handful of requirements, only a minority of which could be called necessities. Likewise motor cars, mobile phones, cameras, home entertainment systems, golf clubs. Communist Russia was the butt of many a Western joke because only one or two of each necessity could be found for sale. This represented the other extreme, fitting nicely into the bleak existence imposed on the poor sods who had to live under such a regime.

The *only reason* our societies have, exponentially, driven out in the other direction is the greed of Profitists, providing pretence choice, pretence competition, by selling the same stuff under a plethora of labels. One example: anti-dandruff shampoo. All but one product (Selsun) contain the same single active ingredient, Zinc Pyrithione, and in the same proportion, 1%WW. Competition? Choice? Bah, humbug.

No alternatives permitted

New Profitism has so completely engulfed the written word, mind content and focus, the airwaves, everyday conversation, whether desires and ambitions are legitimate, whether gains and rewards are legitimate, there is no room left over for other ways of thinking or wanting or hoping or desiring or needing or being satisfied or being frustrated, or anything that is not within the Profitist purview.

Think about it. When was the last time that you gave any serious attention to, or invested anything emotion and feeling in, something other than your mortgage, your debts, your status, the *things* you have and the *things* you want? Or the stresses on your family, your relationships, your thoughts and fears about the future, which are themselves produced by, are the consequence of, the attention and emotions invested in mortgage, debt, status, things?

We can think about, attend to, nothing else because we are all soaking in the marinade of ideas, desires and fears engendered by Profitism. As the Profitists constantly point out, this is the system that *sustains* us, so spend, spend, spend.

And all the while the professional atheists would have us share their anti-religion obsessions, on which they lavish such energy and time – they have the brainpower to do much better – and invite us also to look away from the predations of Profitism and from its consequences. Psychologically, the professional atheists are on a par with the C3s. To which I can only say oh dear, what a waste.

12 THE MARINADE EFFECT

*Well, do you ever get the feeling that the story's
too damn real and in the present . . . tense?
Or that everybody's on the stage, and it seems like
you're the only person sitting in the audience?*

Jethro Tull (Ian Anderson) © *CHRYSALIS MUSIC*

How have we responded to all these assaults on Human
Values?

By slowly losing our own. Let's start with how we have
allowed money to re-define sport.

Sport

With the exception of teams playing for their countries,
sporting teams no longer truly represent tribes or localities
or areas, although the players and the management keep
up a pretence so the fans can still feel involved. The
players, however, are mere mercenaries, mobile and for
hire to the highest bidder. The difference between
sporting contests involving truly representative teams and
those comprising mercenaries is starkly demonstrated in
Australia by the State of Origin Rugby League competition.

The states involved are New South Wales and
Queensland. Players born in those states are spread in
teams Australia-wide throughout a winter competition, but
in State of Origin clashes the representatives *must* have
been born in one state or the other. This is the only
competition between truly representative men's teams I

know of in any code, and is the most fervently played, watched and followed of all the competitions involving the various codes here. Invariably broadcasts of the matches top the TV ratings. In following and barracking for pseudo representative teams, fans are involved, but not as they were in the '40s and '50s, when players had to have a genuine connection with the applicable locality to play for that team. Local loyalty was total. Now it is much weaker.

In the State of Origin competition local loyalty is back. It is an anachronism, where the game and its outcome are more important than any worldly prize. And the people love it. It's real. People in the street discuss the forthcoming match days and weeks before the event. You'd think the powers that be would learn from this, but they are making too much easy money from the competitions involving pretend representative teams. The people are not consciously aware of why one competition is so much more important than the others. The importance is indicated only by their relative degrees of involvement.

Competition and winning

A man I knew well when I first went out on my own as a tame psychologist consultant, gave me excellent advice for succeeding in business, and I did not want to take it and would have been unable to take it anyway. Having watched me win arguments against the insecure and ego-driven boss of an organisation that was giving me quite a lot of work, he took me aside and shocked me with a dichotomy new to me: "Gavin, you're clever but you're not smart." I did not know whether to be chuffed or insulted, not recognising this as an extremely acute distinction. Be clever and win the argument: be smart, and win the contract.

This same man gave me another distinction that was new to me. This was after the one time I 'crewed' for him in a small yacht in a trivial sailing race, this episode also being my first and last sailing experience. He was ferocious in his pursuit of winning, shrieking at me commands like "LEO!!!", which were supposed to mean something to me. When we didn't get close to winning he was very dirty on me. "There are competitors and there are winners, Gavin (biting off the name and nearly spitting). You're a competitor; I'm a winner." How true. At university I once played 'first to 100 wins' at table tennis with a colleague. For months we competed each game ferociously, fighting every point. And neither of us cared who won; the game was the thing. This is not the way to succeed in business. As the man said, winning is the only thing.

Alcohol, drugs and gambling (the Three Banes)

[Tobacco smoking is not included here because the destruction it wreaks directly affects only the body.] There is little, if anything, new I can say on this subject. We all know of the devastating outcomes from addiction to these three blights on society. Their relevance to this book is that each is highly involving of those affected, and is wholly Q3 in nature, ignorant, destructive, mind numbing, spirit-denying. Addiction to any of these produces a Q3 life.

Those who import and control release of the major drugs of addiction stay out of the limelight and are left to get on with their trade. The law comes down hard on the pushers, and in many societies on the users. Where are the owners, importers and distributors? As with all Mister Bigs they are coated in Teflon and known only to each other and to those who protect them. Money talks. It also controls. The billionaire alcohol and gambling controllers, of course, are pillars of society and highly regarded by the public. We swoon over their marriages and weep for their troubles. One of the items in *JobMatch*, the major personality questionnaire I have developed, reads:

> *I admire people who get to the top, no matter how they did it.*

About half of all respondents agree with this statement. *Think about that.*

Few of us have not enjoyed a few drinks or a joint with friends, drinks over dinner, etc, or had a flutter on the races or the pokies. When indulged with a degree of self-control, the enjoyment stays Q2 and a great time is had by all. Q1, of course, is asleep. At the extreme end of 'enjoyment', most illegal drugs induce a sense of freedom, or of power and invulnerability, of joy unalloyed, of bliss; in other words, ersatz liberation and realisation. Drugs cruelly ape the experience which can come, permanently, only through years or decades of hard work and the grace of God. One plus for the addicted: on the way to oblivion the drug-taker is given glimpses of what can be eternally experienced without drugs.

None of the strategies designed to reduce the impact of alcohol consumption and of gambling has succeeded. Each of these curses is eating further and further into the wallets, purses and souls of the population. How, then, have we been so successful in reducing tobacco consumption in the first world? Tobacco is the only bane that is not an addictive substitute for Q1 in our lives. Yes, tobacco is very addictive but all it does is poison us to death. Alcohol, initially, is a lubricant for Q2 activities, fun and games. It is also a dissolver of conscience so the Q2 activities can segue into Q3 pleasures, abandonment of one kind or another, almost without our noticing. In poor buggers with alcoholism tendency genes, the transition goes from sobriety to Q3 without pausing for Q2 in between. Then sobriety is replaced by the craving, and life becomes Q3 drunk or sober. Thus, the alcoholic, who destroys her/himself and all erstwhile relationships.

Gambling is different again. The purpose of the bookmaker, or of the spinning roulette wheel, offering different odds on different horses/ combinations is to suck the gambler looking for Q2 thrills into trying to beat the odds by some presumed skill at doing so. Some individuals, famous in their own milieu, can beat the odds well ahead of chance, leading others to believe that they can acquire this skill. The cleverly constructed odds then keep them coming back and coming back, with most experiencing a blend of Q2 and Q3. The remainder become addicts. These proceed to destroy erstwhile relationships, and frequently themselves.

More recently the Profitists have devised a scrupulously researched and designed method for compelling people, as they drift from Q2 enjoyment through Q3 habit to compulsive addiction, permanent Q3. They have achieved this through the poker machine, known as the one armed bandit in the days when you had to do more than twitch your finger to make the machine perform.

The odds of a win, ranging from a few coins to a jackpot, have been pre-ordained via fine-tuning of the rewards according to intermittent reinforcement theory. If the machine rewarded every, say, tenth button click the house would lose, because everyone would stop playing when they realised they had no choice but to lose. So the trick is to give lots of little rewards, on a seemingly random basis, that give the gambler a feeling of success while keeping the house ahead. Then occasionally comes a jackpot, again perfectly judged so the suckers crouched around the 'winner' feel they have to keep trying – soon it will be their turn.

The intermittent reinforcement odds are perfectly calculated to transmute a sufficiently frequent thrill (Q2) into a permanent Q3 addiction for the predisposed. By then it's not even fun, merely yet another life-destroying dependence. Those who invest in and control gambling venues and opportunities are, whether they realise it or not, doing evil. And – the world champion of cynicism – offering counselling and advice for addicts.

Virtual reality (a rapidly growing fourth bane)

Until recently, virtual reality was seen as something of a gimmick, as were television, the worldwide web and mobile phones in their day. Google 'virtual reality' and you can visit any of the 20,100,000 relevant websites. Google 'Christianity' and you have a choice of 51,200,000 sites. Google 'Buddhism' for 14,700,000. Virtual reality stands up pretty well for level of interest.

One of the leading proponents of VR can be found at secondlife.com. If you visit for the first time, be alarmed and appalled. To be offered a second, virtual life is Profitism at its most insidious and Q3. Not only does it make fortunes for the perpetrators, it keeps Joe and Jane Citizen compliant, quiescent, directed, drugged.

My-Minx

If you would like to see Profitism's greed, propaganda and manipulation at its most blatant and immoral, go to My-Minx on your trusty website. It is aimed at the tweens –

girls aged 9 to 12 - who adopt an avatar, and spend 'pink pounds', which are purchased with real US dollars, on clothes, cosmetic surgery, contraceptives, morning after pills, etc. Of course the more outlandish purchases are more expensive but hey! check in on your avatar's 'happiness level'. The more expensive the purchase the higher the rating on the 'happiness level'. Just another Profitist turn of the screw. 'Bras' are now being marketed to breast-free tweens and younger.

Virtual reality is the true Opium of the People. Karl, where are you now when we really need you?

Cost cutting and lack of interest and care

Nobody cares any more. They haven't the time. The desire to do a good job because it deserves to be done as well as possible has given way to time constraints. Cost is king. Once proud newspapers and magazines are riddled with errors, wrong words and typos, spelling errors, excellent words replaced with totally misleading alternatives by illiterate young sub-editors. Publishers' editors now chop manuscripts around not to clarify and improve the quality and clarity of the writing, but to shorten the work, thus reducing cost. For the same reason, trades people are forced to slash quality in, for instance, cabinet making, as seen in modern kitchens and timber furniture.

Value, valuable

When I was studying at university I once went to a dinner party where the host was a quintessential economic rationalist 30 years ahead of his time. He argued vigorously that nobody ever did anything for motives other than mercenary. This was as true of a nun working for the poor in India as of any Profitist. It did not matter what countervailing examples I threw at him, he swept them aside with the force of his assumptions. I was horrified to find that I could not destroy or even dent his argument: all I could do was say, in effect, I disagree.

Now I am half a century older I realise how prophetic he was. Today, something is of value if its worth in the relevant currency can be established by market forces. No human medical affliction – cancer, asthma, spina bifida – will attract funds from Western governments until its negative outcomes, its value, has been expressed in lost economic production and therefore lost contribution to GDP in dollars. The logic goes, we must do something about halitosis because it is costing the economy, say, $5Bn per year in lost production – people passing out when a colleague breathes on them, etc. We must attend to this problem before we turn to depression and suicide, because this is costing only, say, $3.9Bn per year. The severity and threat of a disease or illness is directly proportional to its economic cost only. Rare diseases will receive only token funds, irrespective of pain and suffering endured.

Speaking of relative values, the US is currently offering a reward of $25M for Osama bin Laden, $13M for another terrorist and $1.2M for yet another. How do they decide the monetary value of a terrorist? How many Americans they've killed? How many hits they get on their website? What Dick Cheney thought about them?

Samuel Johnson, famous for saying patriotism is the last refuge of a scoundrel, in fact was a keen supporter of patriotism, by which he meant love of country. The patriotism he despised is the nationalistic fervour whipped up by those whose other arguments have run dry. If you loved Australia enough you would support its adventures in Vietnam, Iraq and Afghanistan: to fail to do this is to be un-Australian (un-American, un-British, whatever), to demonstrate you don't love your country and everything it stands for. To wave a flag proves that you do.

The Rush

The reason people in modern movies are exploded instead of merely killed is because violence in earlier movies advanced the plot and did not occur as though valuable in its own right. Now violence is not merely gratuitous but is there to produce that rush of adrenalin through the system, that thoughtless wham whack of excitement that is paraded by New Profitism as being the zenith of human experience. This is why the violence found in violent movies comes every five to ten minutes, one rush then another and then another, with the story and characterisation being somewhere between secondary and irrelevant. The immensely popular horror/gore movie genre serves the same function.

As in movies, focus on the rush has also invaded sport. As a cricket tragic I am appalled by the decline of support for test cricket and the rise of the 20/20 form of the game. In between these two extremes lies the one day format, itself an abomination for true lovers of the game's skills, character, strategies and intricacies. A recent survey in India found that among cricket lovers only seven per cent chose test cricket as their preferred form of the game, with the 20/20 version being a mile out in front. New cricket converts think the game comprises batsmen trying to smash the ball out of the ground as often as they can. This produces rush after rush for the spectators, and nothing else.

This cricket transition from a thoughtful, reflective and complicated five day game to a three hour bash and slogfest is a perfect metaphor for how New Profitism has persuaded, cajoled and manipulated us into being happy only when instant gratification – now! – is combined with adrenalin-generating Q2 excitement and pleasure – the rush! This incessant emphasis on having something exciting *now* also helps explain the growth in the numbers of participants in and followers of extreme sports. Likewise gambling of course. All these activities produce rush after rush, that is what they are for.

This coming together of the rush with the win-at-any-cost-winning-is-the-only-thing mentality keeps us as far away as possible from subtlety, reflection, contemplation, all those exercises of the brain that are anathema to New Profitism. If you spend any time thinking you might pause before you buy, if you have time to reflect you might not be sucked in. So everything, if possible, should generate an endless string of rush after rush after rush, and all pleasure comes to be focussed on, defined by, the short lived but extreme and mindless adrenalin rush.

Honesty and integrity

Some years ago I drove into a service station late at night to buy something or other and tendered a $10 note in payment. The assistant gave me the item and the change, and when I returned to the car and made to put the change in my pocket I found I had change of $20. So I went back inside, gave him the $10 note and said he had given me the wrong change. The assistant looked at the note, then looked at me and said, "You're mad ya bastard." Honesty, for him, had become not only unacceptable, but unthinkable. I know such an outlook is more common now than it was in 'my day'. The progressive disappearance of honesty, in the sense of being true to your own conscience, is surely one of the most worrying signs of our society's direction.

Related to this dissolution of honesty is the rise of pragmatic behaviour. Pragmatism has, at base, the assumption that if you can get away with something to your own advantage, well why not. It's only natural. As a leading right wing power broker said, "Whatever it takes." Pragmatism is a key tenet of Profitism.

We are all aware of how honesty has taken a king hit from the powerful in our society. You never hear the word or its synonyms from politicians and business leaders except when they are in full bullshit mode, as in "I place my integrity above everything else." People of true integrity, as with courageous people, do not praise themselves for possessing the qualities they possess. So back to honesty. We all know that in times past you could leave your door unlocked, and your bicycle leaning up against a fence without chain and lock, etc. We also know that back then a majority of people spoke truth a fair proportion of the time, whereas now we are lied to most of the time. Honesty has lost its cachet, has no placed in Profitism. Honesty is a Human Value.

Loyalty

Loyalty has been a much admired and honoured characteristic of dogs and humans for centuries, millennia. Not any more.

For loyalty in its original meaning, *Answers.com* has an excellent definition:

> *Faithfulness or devotion to a person, a cause, obligations, or duties.*

Faithfulness, devotion. Two more words which, in our brave new world order, are losing their content and meaning. Loyalty as a business concept has two meanings. Originally it referred to a marketing orientation based on the belief that if the company did what it said it was going to do, that is, provide an excellent product or service at a fair price, customers would tend to stick with it, that is, be loyal. This concept is close to the word's original meaning.

It has been imperceptibly replaced by the current notion, which is that loyalty can be bought, that is, that people can be bribed, by offers they can't refuse, to remain with the company irrespective of its relative status in the quality and value-for-money stakes. And it works, or they wouldn't do it. Fifteen thousand fly by points if you join us by such a date. Spend a large sum here to get eight cents per litre off when you next fill your tank. And endlessly so on. The cost of all these bribes is, of course, built into the price you pay in the first place. If people stick with the provider only for personal benefit, it is misleading to use the phrase 'loyal customer' to refer to the practice. Surely a better term is sucker. The people suck and the practice sucks.

The age of science?

These have been just some of the outcomes of Profitism *über alles*. With the progressive demise of religion and the rise of science and reason, many believe we are still in the era of science and technology. We are not. We are in the era of consumption, of recklessly purchasing that which is designed to lose its attractiveness because we will always be persuaded that we must have the improved version, or an alternative version with different bells and whistles. Our children's children will not be able to comprehend or believe our stupidity. At least I hope they won't.

All outer, no inner

Against my attack, has not Profitism brought us great benefits? Medical advances aside, benefits yes. Great no. Many have been Q2 in nature, serving passion and activity. The majority have been Q3, relating to greater comfort, diversion and self indulgence. Where are the Q1 benefits, those most readers will have indicated, in <u>Become happy</u>..., are wanted equal to or above all else? Where is the experience of love, contentment, satisfaction in work, contact with nature? Nowhere to be seen, encouraged or experienced. In a society controlled by and run for profit, the ultimate effect on the people is that they are deprived of an inner life. All focus is on the outer, on consumption and self indulgence. This suits Profitism very well.

Increasingly, people are finding themselves disengaged from their work, from each other, and from the person they think they are: and more so from the person they would like to be, and from the life they would like to have. As noted, the word for this state of mind is anomie, generated by alienation.

Gavin Sinclair

13 IS AUSTRALIA CIVILISED?

Is Australia civilised? I am sure that if the population was surveyed with the question "Would you say the English brought civilisation to the natives of Australia?" the majority of (non-indigenous) respondents would say yes. A minority in Australia has condemned the intruders for their obliteration of aboriginal society and culture since the indigenous population was overrun across the Nineteenth Century. Matters are getting worse, ever since the aborigines were placed, about twenty years ago, on permanent welfare handouts and buggerall jobs.

In the absence of influence from any adequate stabilising cultural remnant, aboriginal communities took to drugs and alcohol and paedophilia in a big way. Now the Federal Government has gone in with a big stick to thrash the miscreants into shape. It was mainly a stunt in an election year, of course, but it does exemplify the poverty of familiarity with Human Values that afflicts our politicians. God knows what will happen to these unfortunate human targets. We are, I would say, about as civilised as the United States of America, only without their political and legal safeguards.

The mindset and the heartset

There are very few jobs high up in excitement land, and those who lose out are made to feel failures. Yet just by arithmetic it is *impossible* for all those desiring to rise to levels of power, prestige and wealth to do so. It is like trying to cram a thousand cricket balls into a small bucket. Not one in twenty is going to get in there. This imposes disappointment, disillusionment and alienation among most of our young. A Q3 consciousness is the outcome of life's failures, trials and disappointments.

What have we to offer them? Either (the majority) to feel they have failed, or the successes to lose their humanity and live in constant fear of also losing what they have acquired, McBankBalance, McMansion, McOverdraft, McLimousine, McLifestyle, McSuccess. Their final reward for all that effort? Fear of loss and McSpiritonEmpty. There is always the fear that others will get some of their pie, that they might take it. Profitism, and all the chips off its bleak block, teach that success is measured in eye-catching consumption, in Q2 activities and Q3 indulgence.

Those born into or who emigrated into such a failure-generating society, and who 'lose', can choose either to accept their fate of lowly and low paid jobs or no jobs at all, poor health, rotten amenities and services, and so on; or they can follow rebellious leaders who may have their own violence-loving agenda, but who say the things the desperate and hopeless long to hear. You are important, you are being ignored or treated like shit by those with the wealth and power. They take what *they* want. It's time we did the same. Think Hitler. Thus arise the gangs, and the drunken hopeless violent ones outside the pubs and clubs, the no-go zones, the gated communities provided to resist the violent behaviour of the alienated and to protect privilege.

Stroll through the poison on the internet designed to stimulate, titillate, arouse lust and generate delicious violence fantasies. See the 'action' movies the kids watch, created for them by the same exploitative system. Play the video games, especially those involving 'first person shooters'. Enjoy the child porn on the web. Click on the latest virtual sex and violence websites. It all exists, we are told, because we must worship three gods: freedom of enterprise, freedom of choice and market forces. Besides, you can't blame what they watch for what they do. We now see where all this bullshit we have been sold has brought us.

Here is the modern mindset. The word heartset would probably do as well.

we must win, succeed, acquire;

we must fear loss of these because there is only so much room at the top, and there are many who would topple us if and when they can;

we know that our present source of success and acquisition, our job, can at any time be extinguished; and

there are millions of the envious and barbaric 'out there' across the sea who are aching to take it from us;

we must have no concern for those who fail in these endeavours;

it is quite OK to take advantage of another's misfortune or weak position – the 'if I didn't someone else would' justification;

when these losers 'play up' and cause anything from a nuisance to a riot, we must come down on them with the full force of our righteousness; and

all who promote Human Values may be admirable and all that crap, but we must not let them distract us from our goal; and only action, excitement, violence and sex can provide the satisfactions necessary to round out the McLifeStyle existence.

Hear Mic Looby on this. [None of Your Business, The Big Issue, No 282, p12.]

I had an awful nightmare last week. I dreamed that Australia's major political parties merged with Australia's biggest corporations. But that wasn't the worst of it. The worst of it was, nobody noticed...

Teenagers stopped thinking about sex altogether and instead became obsessed with property speculation. Mum and dad investors were selling their children and then buying them back again once their value had dropped. This wasn't dog eat dog. It was dog set up cheap off-shore company to sell dog meat back to dog and then diversify before the market crashes due to an over-supply of half-eaten dog. ...

I wish I'd written that.

My prejudices

Cooler presentations of facts outlined here and in the previous chapter have been tried on doubters for decades, and the Profitists have ignored them. The best Australian example is political economist Ted Wheelwright, who since the 1960s from Sydney University pinpointed the future of global Profitism, that is, our present experience of Super Capitalism, with error-free accuracy.

Not all of the world's worst anti-Human-Values excesses arise from unbridled Profitism. Zimbabwe demonstrates what a mad despot can achieve against the citizens if he really tries. The People's Republic of China is rocketing into the Profitist mindset, but in addition is driving poor people out of Beijing for reasons of crass nationalism, so the capital will present to the world a pristine city. My concern is with Western societies.

I have not written this representation of Profitism so ardently to anger or even to sting the apologists and supporters, nor to warm those who feel as I do. It's just the way I feel. True, I want to leave the apologists little room for denial, but if you re-read this exposition and extract the fervour, you will be left with detached reality.

By way of balance, here is another of my prejudices: I believe the human spirit is ever ready to stir into action, a tap waiting to turn on. This explains how our exploited and anxious young can rise to any occasion immediately after they have refused to give you their seat in the bus. It is often said the future of the world is in safe hands. So it is, so long as we don't wreck it first, or drive the young even further into a world of their own.

I hope to stir, in thinking people much younger than myself, who have been given so little to think about by our decision makers, a degree of insight and concern sufficient to encourage them to feel, correctly, that only they can do something to reverse our slide into God knows what. That is my wish, made in the full knowledge that God could well have entirely something else in train of which I am ignorant.

Conclusion

To blame the excesses of Profitism for the Western world's woes and for many of those in the second and third worlds is unfashionable. Where would the world be without it? One thing we do know; where the world is with it, and not only with it but *because* of it.

Yours fatally, Profitism

Please give some time, right now, to trying to think of any viable alternative explanation, any cause for the effects we see around us other than the logic, performance and excesses of Profitism. If you can do so you are cleverer than I am. I am going to assume you cannot come up with an alternative, and that you therefore share, however reluctantly, the arguments I have presented so far.

14 SUMMARY OF PURPOSE

The reason we keep on doing what we've always done is because nothing *effective* has intervened in our lives to encourage or make us change. To repeat a powerful truism from <u>Become happy</u>...:

If you keep on thinking what you've always thought, you'll keep on doing what you've always done.

If you keep on doing what you've always done, you'll keep on getting what you've always got.

So, if you want to change what you get, you must change what you think and therefore what you do.

As every parent knows, lectures and appeals to children make little or no difference. As parents also know, being told that their own slackness and incompetence are the cause of the wildness and out-of-controlness of youth today is politics-serving rubbish. Does anyone ask why the parents are helpless to bring about the changes they and the society at large – excepting the young, of course – want to see happen? They do not. Our society is afraid to drill down beyond the easy 'responsibility' targets of parents or 'soft' law enforcement and into the murky forces unbridled Profitism has brought to bear. We change when the forces upon us change – forces to help us see a better way, and/or forces that are going to make us change anyway.

Re-arranging the forces upon us

No-one can blame Profitism alone for making the most of our overwhelming preference for that which glitters and is not gold, our 24/7 illusion, and our enthusiastic response to its appeal and magnetism. Those who pursue non-Profitist ends, and particularly if they live a life based upon Human Values precepts, are of no use to those in power anywhere or, so far, at any time. They are too pure, as in unsullied, not riddled with crap.

All focus on Human Values has been successfully opposed by whichever system has been in power and influence at the time, dictatorship, communism, socialism, and Profitism until quite recently. It is only over the past couple of decades that Profitists have gone further, have come to realise that the path to their own everlasting happy hour is through filling our minds so completely with Profitism's attractions and rationale there is literally no room left over for contemplation of other principles.

The essence of spirituality

All that spirituality means is making friends with your spirit, not spirits out there, but yours, you, the real inner Self. We can, easily or with difficulty, get in touch with our thoughts, our feelings, our emotions, our bodies and bits of our bodies. None of these is yourself. Only your spirit, your soul, is you. You know that. From time to time you feel it and are aware of it. Meditation is the Cupid that brings our awareness and our Self together with love. Spirituality is the deepening contact between these two, and love is not effeminate, dorky, wussy, weak, or soft.

Being a male myself, and having talked with thousands of men over the past many years, I am very aware that men, including many 'believers', become most uncomfortable when considering or talking about meditation and spirituality. Even well before Profitism decided to replace our minds, spirituality and spirit were definitely considered rather effeminate, nerdy, weak, soft concepts. Real men might, if starving, eat quiche, but they were definitely not spiritual.

I have tried to overcome such a possible reaction throughout this book and Become happy ... by emphasising what you have probably discovered for yourself; that you desire an increase in Q1 experiences in your life, and a steady diminution in Q3 pursuits. But it's still not quite enough, is it? There is still the lingering feeling, if not certainty, if you are a male, that matters of the spirit are somehow unmanly.

All I can do is assert – manly men meditate: swallow your pride and your ego long enough to discover that you can be masculine and spiritual. Among men, this combination exemplifies the perfect spiritual warrior. Fortunately for women they are not, in general, afflicted with the self puffing up we men seem prey to. Women may still reject God and spirituality of course, but their reasons are likely to be less predictable and more personal.

The mind

The mind does only one thing: it thinks. It juggles information and memories and stimulus input and reaches conclusions or worries about not knowing which conclusion to choose and on and on. If you have a good and a strong and, particularly, a pure mind it can be a great servant. If it is confused and loaded down with ignorance and prejudices it can be a beast of a master. The mind can make contact with and play with ideas endlessly, but the one thing it cannot do is make contact with the soul, the Self. Only if such contact becomes prevalent, preferably near universal, we will not halt the world's descent into misery.

Until we have been awakened out of our unconsciousness, our mind can no more come to grips with the Self within than it can think in any way usefully about God 'out there' in the sky. To know the Self we must quiet the mind and all its manipulations, and the only practice which can achieve this is some form of meditation, because meditation is the only road to knowledge that ignores the mind, in fact renders it temporarily silent.

By definition, any practice which stills the chatter of the mind, and damps down arousal, while we are still alert and awake, is a meditation practice. Therefore, every one of us has meditated. Some meditate by gardening, or by fishing, or by lying on their back watching the clouds form and reform. The reason it makes sense to learn more formal meditation practices is so we can meditate whenever we want to, and are not limited to a particular activity or surrounding.

Once you are a regular meditator you will experience flashes of awareness, of *unmesha*, flashes of realisation that you are on the right path.

Desire for cooperation and community

Probably since the cave, human survival has involved people drifting or deliberately gathering into groups of some kind, in which participants are dedicated towards shared activities or goals, or at least to the integrity and maintenance of the group. This is so unchallengeably evident it does not need spelling out here. There is also no need to argue – because the evidence is there for all to see – that most aspects of 'community' in Western society are breaking down. Neighbours used to chat on the street or over the fence. Now they don't even know each others' names, and avoid contact if possible. This is particularly true of medium and high density housing, now overtaking all cities.

The power of meditation

Nothing is helping us move away from selfish individuality towards community, sharing and cooperation. Meditation can do this. Meditation is the alchemy that allows us gradually to drop our obsessions, compulsions, dogmatic certainties, self-centred desires and self justifications, and to replace them with positive Q1 orientations. We gain access to the inner knowledge we all share, and which to most of us has so far been a completely unknown quantity. We have no inkling that it is there, waiting for us. Meditation does not make anything happen: it simply allows us to tap into our own inner knowledge and wisdom, which then, also gradually, automatically guide us in our choices, decisions and actions. The mind takes a back seat, looking after the everyday. This is a beautiful process, generating an energy, a buzz, which is shareable, catching. I recommend it.

15 A PRACTICE OF MEDITATION

This is almost a duplicate of chapter 20 from <u>Become happy</u>.... It is as close as I can come to introducing meditation as a daily practice, and to fiddle with it to make it 'different' would be phoney and without purpose. It is included here for those who have not read the earlier book. It includes some new material

Here, first, are the practicals, those things that are worth doing in order to start off with the best possible chance of developing a useful practice using any technique.

First, early on

Decide to meditate at least five days per week.

Decide on a place where you will meditate. Later, you will be able to meditate wherever you like, but start by building up your meditation energy in one place.

Your meditation space or spot, ideally a room but few of us have that luxury these days, must be quiet, clean and uncluttered, out of 'foot traffic lanes', which build up an energy you don't need. Turn your mobile phone off and disconnect a landline from the wall.

Sit for meditation with something pleasing in front of you – an image of someone divine if you like, or a photograph of something or somewhere you love, a lit candle or a vase, definitely not a boring blank wall or corner.

Sit on a cushion on the floor if that suits you and you are flexible with a strong back: otherwise in a reasonably upright chair with good lumbar support, and with your back straightish but not stiff.

Sit quietly with your eyes open for awhile, chatting to yourself about how you are sitting for meditation, and how you are going to relax and enjoy yourself. Your fundamental wish is to close the gap between your familiar self and your Self.

Have your hands on your knees or thighs, or lightly clasped in your lap.

And meditate

Close your eyes and start to breathe comfortably. As you relax, breathe as slowly as you can without forcing the issue.

Be very aware of your breathing, how smooth and comforting it is, how regular, how essential to your wellbeing.

With each out-breath, relax your body, not into a slump but as though you realise your body could be heavier, as though your bottom is going to press more heavily down onto the earth/cushion/chair. In this way use your breath to relax your eyes and face and neck and arms and stomach and thighs. You are getting heavier. Just think of these parts of your body as you breath in and out – you do not need to go into a deep relaxation routine.

Remind yourself of why you are meditating. You wish to develop – and silently touch them with your mind – patience, love, generosity, courage, and any other desired characteristics as they occur to you. Say each one silently on an out-breath. Do this as you settle down and then taper the words off as you relax more.

Keep mentally watching your breathing, feel gratitude for the breath. Then, for the first week or two of your practice, mentally say, on each outbreath, any word that will help you into a state of relaxation, such as "relax", "peace", "love".

Then for the next couple of weeks – don't rush it! – say, "I", followed by the word '"am". Silently say "I" on the in-breath and "am" on the out-breath, so the emphasis is on the am. Not I am happy, or I am loving, or I am wealthy, just "I . . am". My reasoning here is that we are so many things; I am a psychologist, I am a father, I am a husband, I am a telemarketer, I am Caucasian, I am intelligent, I am selfish, we can go on forever. No wonder we're so confused about our true nature.

We are not practising affirmations. "I AM" is not a whistle in the dark: it is a statement of our true nature. Say it with conviction. Don't shout it in your head, simply mean it, know it is true. "I think, therefore I am" is crap. Thinking is irrelevant, even misleading. You are. Assert it.

If your mind intrudes, chatter, chatter, let it fade and stop, as though you were talking and decide slowly to stop. Don't listen to it; do not get caught up in what it might be saying. Then return to your breath and "I . . . am".

It does not matter if you miss a few repetitions and simply breathe in and out: when this happens, watch and enjoy the breath. You may find you want to stop thinking the words altogether: this is good; let them drop. Alternatively, you may find the word repetition a little tense-making or intruding on your relaxation – i.e., it seems like an effort. If so, return to watching your breath: be aware of its passage in and out. You can return to the words in later meditations.

The breath

A good exercise with the breath is to think of the tip of your nose as a point of equilibrium between in here and out there. Watch your breath as it comes in and see it zooming through and into every part of your body – the in-breath goes into every corner. Then the out-breath sweeps out, flowing out through the entire universe. In into the entire inner universe, out off to the entire outer universe. This is a wonderful settling, steadying and centering technique.

Eternal infinity lies in those small spaces between the end of the inbreath and the start of the outbreath, and between the end of the outbreath and the start of the inbreath.

Meditate once a day, preferably at the same quiet time, and for between ten and twenty minutes, depending on how you feel about it. Lengthen the time gradually at a pace that suits you. If you take to meditation like the proverbial duck to water, beware overdoing it: do not exceed one hour.

A reminder: do not be alarmed, or conclude that you have been asleep, if you find you have 'passed out' when your meditation period concludes. This is not sleep, it is tandra, a state of higher consciousness between sleeping and waking.

It's OK to use an alarm of some sort to bring yourself out, but don't use an analogue clock with a real bell:

you want to come out of meditation gently, not by driving your head up into the ceiling.

As you get used to it

Now, as you drop into your meditation routine, remind yourself that you wish to establish contact with your inner Self, your true nature which resides in the heart.

Once settled and relaxed and starting your meditation with "I . . .am", start to say "I am (. . . [one of] . . . love, courage, kindness, compassion, patience)". Start with "love", and remember, you are not addressing your little self, who may not be super loving at all. You are acknowledging your Self, so you can say "I am love" with complete confidence and without any hypocrisy or embarrassment at all. Silently say the "I am" on the in-breath, and "love" on the out-breath. Do not merely say the words "I am love" to yourself, feel the love, know you are love, for you are; your Self is love and everything that flows from love.

Keep "I am love" going for a week or two, or for as long as you like, remembering to let the words fade away as your meditation becomes deeper, then spend a week or two keeping the "I am" going on the in-breath and adding different Q1 descriptors as time goes by: courage, persistence, generosity, whichever Q1 characteristics you fancy.

N.B. Not 'I am courageous', or persistent, or generous or loving. You are acknowledging the Self, so use the noun, not the adjective – use 'I am courage', 'I am persistence', 'I am generosity'. **Feel** each one as you say it to yourself.

These seem like affirmations, but go much further because you are not trying to make yourself into a new person by this means. You are not seeking to change your personality for the better: you are acknowledging and recognizing what you already are, your true nature, and by this process you are reminding yourself of this fact. You are recognizing yourSelf, and by some process of spiritual osmosis the qualities will progressively penetrate your daily life.

Regularly re-read

You will, naturally, forget components of the above, and in doing so might go off on an undesirable tangent. Until you get used to the process it is a good idea, perhaps once every two weeks, to re-read the above guide to meditation immediately before you settle into your preferred position.

As time goes by

I am not saying it is up to you, that if you give it a good shot beautiful things will happen. I hope they do, but the whole thing is quite out of our hands. We sit for meditation, then God takes over. Meditation is not something we *do*. It is something we allow to happen, and once we give ourselves to meditation we are in the most fundamental of 'over to you' situations. Do not expect quick, spectacular results. Nevertheless, you will almost certainly notice, with the passage of time, that the following occur. You will...

Yours fatally, Profitism

gradually increase your Q1 experiences;

equally gradually, find Q3 activities less appealing;

find stresses less stressful;

sleep better;

be less anxious;

increase your creativity;

increase your self confidence;

have more mental clarity;

be more energetic;

find bodily afflictions less pressing;

find that things that bother you bother you less;

come to decisions more quickly, such that eventually you

come to decisions without thinking about them;

have more energy and tire less quickly;

generally find that everything is easier, smoother, less trouble;

and that

you are happier and more at peace.

Gavin Sinclair

16 THE CHOICE IS OURS

There has never been a period in human history when so much hangs in the balance between what is and what might be, when so much depends on the choices we make as individuals, when it is so clear that we are, each of us, 'decision-makers' in deciding the destiny of humankind. It is a time, then, that offers so much meaning. And yet, because of the pressures, preoccupations and priorities of life today, we don't sense the significance of this moment – or sensing it, seem unable to hold it or be inspired by it. Recognising this can help us make the right choices – and so find more meaning in our lives and improve our well-being.

Richard Eckersley, 2004. <u>Well and Good</u>,

Text Publishing, Melbourne, pp 7-8.

So what can we do to improve our society and our world, a question asked by many and answered by many, and here we still are, in the pits. Recent research in Australia has found that a large majority is optimistic about the future, a view shared by Australia's leading social researcher, Hugh McKay. In the light of everything I have written in this book, such optimism, unsupported by mechanisms to right the wrongs, is whistling in a dark wood on a moonless night. I hope they are right. I believe they will be proved right, but only if we can somehow neutralise the grossest impacts of Profitism, those influences which are more of an enemy to the human race than the actions of all extremists and fundamentalists combined. These impacts are spirit denying, life denying.

Only global heating can compare with unbridled Profitism as an avoidable challenge.

Where are we now?

Profitists and their supporters can think highly rationally in areas affecting their profits and advancement: without such brilliant head work we would not have the onward march of technology. But that's it! Their thinking can come to no rational conclusions about society, culture, family, friendship, social cohesion, ecology, environment, etc, for two reasons. First, lack of interest: these matters do not provide the kinds of benefits the Profitists and the brain washed desire. The second reason their thinking goes nowhere on these Human Values matters arises from the first. Their indifference generates crazy assumptions about such concerns; e.g., we can win hearts and minds by killing people we disapprove; by asserting that global warming is not happening, or if it is, that it is just another swing of the geological time pendulum. It is not their arguments or their reasoning that is insane, it is their outlandishly erroneous assumptions. This is why I say and have proven they are crazy. They will see us all dead, but will not see their hand in it at all. So, how to reverse this ecological/environmental, this ecovironmental catastrophe?

What can we do about Profitism?

At last, decision-making reader, we come to making choices. These are the possibilities on offer:

Gavin Sinclair

A. Go along for the ride

Keep going as now, and see what happens. One of the main aims of this book is to demonstrate that such a response would condemn our descendants to nothing less than environmental, societal, cultural and personal degradation and devastation. Anomie will be your contribution to the outcome if you put this book aside thinking, interesting argument but let's just see what happens.

B. Drop out, go feral

Go hippie or feral. OK, if that's what you want. Be aware that in doing so you would be as useful to our successors as will be all those, probably a majority of well intentioned people in the world as it is, who choose alternative A.

C. Take to the guns and streets

In the USSR, and the rest of the one-time Eastern bloc, force overcame power structures which were either feudal or Profitist. And look what happened to them. China, Vietnam and Laos overcame Profitist regimes, and at least in the case of the first two are now scrambling madly to clasp Profitism and the Profitists to their bosom. If you can't beat them, become them. If any group in First World countries tried revolution – a la the Bader Meinhoff experiment in Germany – they would be crushed. Forget it.

D. Campaign against Profitism

This is to campaign actively, from peaceful protests to stamping the feet in anger, against Profitism in any or all

134

of its manifestations. As they always have, such efforts will come to nothing.

What have Michael Moore's confronting documentaries achieved in outcomes? Most people do not see the injustice and exploitation underlying the Profitist ethic, so peaceful protests will be ignored, violent protests will be crushed. There will be no popular support or uprising. Keep in mind always that the essential purpose of all law enforcement agencies is the protection of wealth and property and of those who own them. You will have seen Sydney in APEC lockdown as $150M was spent to ensure that the 21 world leaders did not hear people saying nasty words. You will also have seen similar mighty force brought against protesters in the context of G8 meetings designed to 'improve', to soften, Profitism.

E. Try to change it from within

Join in the Profitists' agenda and mechanisms, playing the game while simultaneously hoping to work from within to humanise and soften the impacts. Profitism and Human Values cannot coexist in any way that will advance Human Values. Profitism will always win. Forget it.

F. Do good works

Become involved in doing good works yourself, maybe in the classical areas historically covered by charities, or in the growing area of cultural creativity, within which there are many individuals and groups tackling and trying to reframe the influences on us in a way that makes more sense than in the past. This book is a contribution to such reframing, and if you wish mainly to be involved in charitable work good luck to you – it's good karma.

G. Rely on reason and argument

Turn, as for example does atheist Michel Onfray, to philosophical and rational approaches to solving humanity's problems. In our post modernist, values-free cultural environment, these are likely to be even less influential and effective than they were when the Enlightenment ruled unchallenged. This is pissing into the wind and taking pride in the spray.

H. Meditate for spiritual development

In Become happy..., I argued and demonstrated that meditation is the only path guaranteed to take us towards Self knowledge and the development of the life we want, one filled with Q1 experiences. Here they are, reproduced from that book:

contented, joyful, loving, fearless, generous, peaceful, faithful, insightful, kind, cheerful.

A meditation revolution is the only approach not yet tried, the approach to change in which you do the best you can to grow in Self knowledge and in a life more designed to attract Q1 experiences and to diminish Q3 indulgences, at a pace and in steps that suit you. As your knowledge grows and as you grow in love and self respect and confidence your example will automatically have an increasingly beneficial effect on those you deal with and on others around you.

Your response to the excesses of Profitism? Here are the choices in summary.

Yours fatally, Profitism

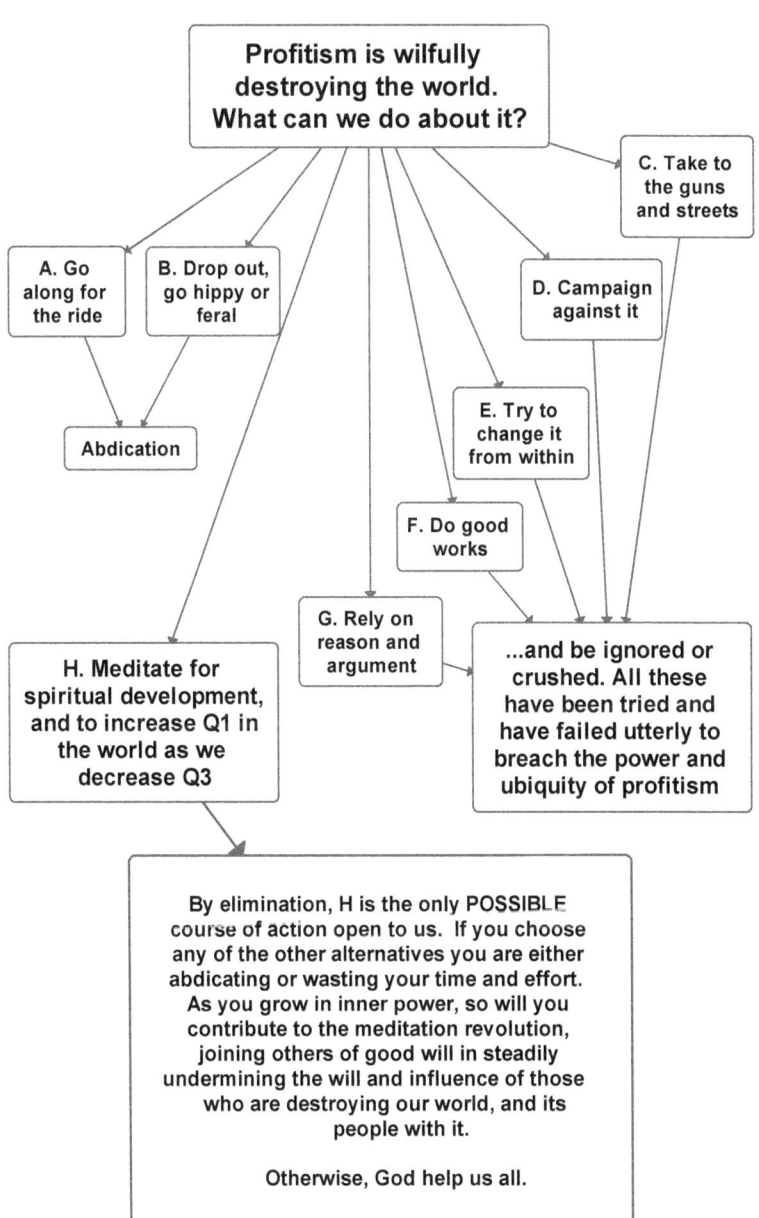

Profitism is wilfully destroying the world. What can we do about it?

C. Take to the guns and streets

A. Go along for the ride

B. Drop out, go hippy or feral

D. Campaign against it

Abdication

E. Try to change it from within

F. Do good works

G. Rely on reason and argument

H. Meditate for spiritual development, and to increase Q1 in the world as we decrease Q3

...and be ignored or crushed. All these have been tried and have failed utterly to breach the power and ubiquity of profitism

By elimination, H is the only POSSIBLE course of action open to us. If you choose any of the other alternatives you are either abdicating or wasting your time and effort. As you grow in inner power, so will you contribute to the meditation revolution, joining others of good will in steadily undermining the will and influence of those who are destroying our world, and its people with it.

Otherwise, God help us all.

17 THE MIND HAS FAILED US

Where the world is now is the direct result of the misdirecting minds of the powerful and the wealthy over the past 100 years. Each of us knows that our best decisions have come about because they *felt* right, not because they were the product of coolly applied intellect. The mind, plural, has failed us, and therefore we must come to rely on the heart, on our intuition, free from the mind's guidance and control. Although meditation is the answer, we must not tell ourselves that we are meditating to bring about some outcome we *think* is appropriate. We must keep the mind not only open but *out of it*.

Don't meditate for a particular outcome

I hope you are persuaded that *something* must be done. Although there must be a viable alternative to Profitism or our future is bleak indeed, we should beware planning what the world would be *like*, how our societies would be *structured*, if Profitism lost its strangling grip on minds and hearts.

If you decide to take the meditation route, it is essential not to expect too much too soon, or to expect anything in particular. We can have only ego-driven, or at best, well-meaning and ideology-serving ideas of what such a world could or should be like.

Additionally, people with the best will in the world will differ markedly from each other in what they see as desirable, not so much in the Human Values sense, on which I suspect all will agree, but when they try to imagine the ideal structure for a changed society, and the functions which would support it. To show you what I mean, here are a few of my suggestions:

1. If we are to do anything to change the world, one of the places to start is to focus on denial and deception. For example, politicians keep saying that the West should do more to encourage moderate Muslims to take on, weed out, the extremists in their ranks. Why should they, when their view of what the West is doing to Muslim states is much closer to the view of the extremists than it ever will be to the view of the C3s. What they do not share with the extremists is the commitment to random violence. If the West fails to deal with the sources of Muslim frustration and anger (favouring Israel over Muslim states at all times and under all circumstances; occupying Muslim lands; dealing with Muslims worse than with animals, à la Abu Graib), extremism can only rise. Look at how successful it has been so far, in Iraq, in Afghanistan, in the US, in the UK, in Pakistan, in Indonesia. The more they rattle and damage the West and its dependent states, the more they will pursue the same policy and practices. Why should they change? The US is standing in the middle of a growing ants' nest wielding a sledge hammer. The more ants it crushes the more ants spring up and bite.

2. Moves towards a focus on fairness and equity: why are fines, either from court outcomes or by regulation, as in traffic and parking fines, not means tested? A $77 fine for staying beyond a parking time limit, is nothing to the well off, and is a crippling blow to, for example, the working poor and pensioners. Here is a suggestion which, although unfair in its own right, would be more just. Start with small fines for all for a first offence, say, $10. This would be nothing to the wealthy and would be a wake up

call for those with little money. Fines for subsequent offences would increase as per recent taxable income, with fines for the rich taking off astronomically, so they will notice, and modestly for the poor, so they will also notice, but manage. Moves towards a fairness focus such as this would greatly reduce alienation and resentment in the community, with flow-on downward impacts on crime levels in various categories.

3. For the time being keep all current laws designed to curb hoonish, thuggish and anti social behaviour, while simultaneously taking steps towards the development of a more equitable and socially concerned society. Retaining and implementing the present anti-underclass laws would silence the anti-bleeding-heart brigade, the shock jocks and the fascist politicians, while real advances could be made towards reducing the social conditions which generate the unacceptable behaviour in the first place.

4. There must be a big role for music in all procedures and practices designed to advance what Baba Muktananda called the meditation revolution. I read somewhere that, in areas frequented by 'thugs', 'hoons' and other undesirables, the playing of Mozart, or any classical music, over a good quality PA system drove them away. God knows what it would do to them if they played Bach. Rather like the vampire and the cross, or the zombie and garlic. It seems their capacity even to respond to a Q1 experience has been destroyed or, let us hope, anaesthetised by their life experiences. I am convinced music could play a big role in bringing them back to themSelves.

5. The churches must become more active. To recognise how far the Churches have taken us from the experience of God is not to ignore or to deny their proper role, which Kevin Rudd wrote was, and this is worth

repeating, "... to give power to the powerless, voice to those who have none, and to point to the great silences in our national discourse where otherwise there are no natural advocates." Some religious spokespeople do this, most do not.

6. [per favour Wendy Sinclair] Many in influential positions in Christian churches meditate now, as do monks and many priests and nuns. The churches could make an immense contribution to desirable change if they taught meditation to parishioners. They could have five minutes of meditation at the conclusion of services; could teach meditation at Sunday School, etc. Children love meditating.

7. **All** government pensions and allowances should be means tested.

See? Already there would be people arguing with me about what is and is not desirable in these suggestions, tempers might rise, others would put forward their views, and suddenly we would find ourselves carrying on in a knowledge vacuum. None of us knows what is coming. If we humans decide to do so we can turn around the alienation from God which underlies the state we are in, but as to the specifics of what a better world would be like we can only argue and bicker, or wait and see. Not only because we can have no idea, but because efforts to play Clever Dick and see who was the best predictor – which is certainly what would happen – would distract us from our own spiritual growth. Besides which, it would be fun to see where God takes us when we are really trying.

We all have courage in there

Much or most of the time we are self centred, selfish to some degree, wary if not frightened, and so on. In the right circumstances, however, we can behave totally 'out of character'. When do we throw all this self absorption aside and call up and practise our good side? When there is an emergency, from saving people from a burning house to coping with a tsunami, an earthquake or a military invasion. Mates in warfare show incredible selflessness and courage in looking after each other. Almost invariably, when people are asked how they found the courage to dash into a burning house to drag strangers to safety, or to win the VC by single handedly wiping out half a dozen enemy machine gun nests, or to carry out any other act requiring courage way out of the ordinary, they say: "I didn't have time to think, really, I just did it. Anyone would have."

This is not false modesty. "Just did it" is the clue. No time for our egos to crash in yelling look out, you're in danger, don't be a fool, don't do it, you'll *die*. Well, if the little self did not do it, who did? Right, the Self. God in action, however briefly, with you in the saddle without the reins. In the everyday, most of us have no access to God within. In addition, most of us are cowards when we have the *time* to panic, or to worry about ourselves or our reputation. In extremis, if given no time to panic or assess the impact the situation could have on *us*, God within acts for us by *being* us. Recall Baba Muktananda's constant reminder to his followers, "Your God dwells within you as you".

The sad part about this is that we seem unable to call up such courage and freedom from self-awareness at will. We are too caught up in what will people think, and will I look OK doing this, and it's not my business let them look after themselves, and all the other ego-iferous bullshit we allow to guide and control our lives. If – ideal case – we all meditated, and started to live more from our Self than from our ego, we would not need the surprise event to bring out the best in us. We would simply behave with more courage, conviction and appropriateness. Poor behaviour, including among those nominally pursuing spiritual development, would decrease.

If we are to turn this planet around, we must do something on a large scale not yet seriously practised by humanity. Some say let's get the good people into power, and they'll do all the right things. That, alone, would never do the trick, besides which it would never happen. The good people are nowhere near as one-pointed and determined as are the bad and the self-serving. The good would be crunched before they got close to applying widespread influence. Utopia is a wet dream if we think it can be brought about by human effort alone.

Many have taken a band of idealistic and well meaning followers and tried to set up a model mini society. In the 19th century about 500 Australians tried to found a truly socialist society in Patagonia. The hard environment and their human natures beat them in no time, and the attempt folded. An abundance of well meaning idealism achieves nothing in the absence of strong decision makers and people willing to do the boring, difficult and repetitive society-maintaining work, such as building, storing, distributing, keeping records and so on. Forget political idealism. Let us stay with meditation as a potential solvent of our less desirable tendencies, those aspects of our nature to which we wish to kiss goodbye.

A word on atmosphere

I left my home state at the age of twenty nine, and after two years in Canberra was offered a position at the

University of New South Wales, so drove down to Sydney in advance to suss the place out. I loved it, I was knocked out. Which is what I said, in the staff tearoom on my return, in reply to the question what do you think of Sydney. I then added that the place had the feel of a big city, to which a behaviourist colleague murmured the query, dripping with positivistic sarcasm, "And how would you measure that feel?" This was my first personally distinct and absolutely clear introduction to the distinction between psychologists interested in human nature and the human condition and psychologists interested only in what people do, which is so much easier to articulate and to measure accurately. And in the world's academies the writing was already on the wall that only the latter approach would survive. Psychology is now just as caught up in the Profitist ethic as are all the other highly paid professions. Do I say that because I never made enough money myself? Good heavens, *no*!

Some years ago my wife and I had an intelligent and sensitive kelpie cross dog, Pog. He went everywhere with us in the back of the car, giving us quick little tongue kisses fair in the mouth if we turned around to say G'day. One early evening we were approaching a country town in Queensland where we intended to fill up with petrol. There were a few people milling around but nothing out of the ordinary. I don't know who started it, Pog or us, but Wendy and I suddenly felt uncomfortable and nervous: the place felt so hostile. Simultaneously, Pog started to growl, deep and threatening, sounding twice his size, which he had never done before and never did again. I turned around and his hackles were well and truly up, his teeth were completely bare, also never seen before or since, and he slowly swivelled his head from side to side, raking everything with a hard stare. We decided to wait until the next opportunity for petrol and Pog kept up the performance until we were out of town.

Whether we can measure it or not, humans and human activities generate energy, vibrations. This is not New Age bullshit. Physics has now acknowledged that nothing is solid or liquid at all; everything is energy. Even the hardest rock or length of steel is, at its innermost reality, a dazzling whirl of infinitesimal bits or energies, not solid at all, seeming solid only because of the intense attraction of the micro energetic forces to each other.

Be in a football crowd enjoying a home game at some critical stage – is there not energy to be felt in addition to the noise level? Does the energy not change when the siren ends the game just before the opponents have an opportunity to take the lead? And how different is the energy if the opponents take the lead just before the siren sounds, and win? Walk into any great cathedral when few are present. Is there not an energy to feel, a peace and stillness rarely experienced in daily life? Be on the fringe of a crowd turning into a vengeful mob. Again, a tangible and frightening energy, even if we can't measure it. Energies and energy change are everywhere.

The Chinese know all about this, the yin and the yang, Feng Shui. Walk around a leafy, upper middle class suburb and tell me the atmosphere, the feel, is no different from that experienced in a down market, mainly poor immigrant suburb, or even more so, a suburban area peopled by the so-called underclass. Walk into a nursing home for the dementing and tell me it feels the same as an equally quiet meditation session.

Or take one place, your favourite place in the world, a particular beach or lake, mountain scenery, a place in the desert or the bush, a city or town. Of such a place we are likely to say how we love its changing moods, one day or one time of day still and peaceful, another boiling with activity, today blue tomorrow grey. How do these same places have their differing impact? Look at photographs taken during the differing moods and we recall only ghosts of the true moods, the true feeling. As the quip goes, you had to be there. Energy is everything and everything is energy.

Let's change the *Zeitgeist*

Think of a family you know which is constantly on the financial edge, where tension is present most of the time and the members argue and bicker with fear, resentment and buck passing. Or think of meeting up with a couple where one has just discovered the other has been unfaithful. As you enter the room they try hard to appear normal. In either case, we are likely to say afterwards you could have cut the atmosphere with a knife.

If we join people who have just suffered the painful loss of a loved one, we are subdued, we may not share but we can feel their pain. Every family, every group, every city has its own atmosphere, its own feel. This may change as circumstances change, but if the *dominant* people behave and influence others in certain ways, so will the group take on an inevitable mood, atmosphere and outlook. When this atmosphere, this spirit, is ubiquitous across a nation or the world for a reasonable length of time, we refer to this holistic experience as the Zeitgeist, the spirit of the age.

Germany's inter-war experience

Consider Germany between the two world wars. Initially, after a crushing defeat and subsequent wretched humiliation, the Zeitgeist comprised poverty, shame, humiliation, hopelessness, anger, directionlessness. Scrabbling efforts at democracy repeatedly failed and then along came a little corporal who said follow me and I will make you not only strong again but invincible. Very tasty, and an overwhelming majority did just that. With well known exceptions, the spirit of the people rose and rose and the Zeitgeist of confidence, arrogance and invincibility became established. This amazing change in cultural confidence, including the reversal of earlier characterising components, took place over a fifteen year period. Hitler, through the force of his personality and a magnificent propaganda machine, changed the minds and the spirits of the people such that they became a totally different nation.

We must do something like this about the Profitist Zeitgeist, but its slow demise cannot be achieved by a Hitler or by any form of frontal attack, material sabotage, inspirational Human Values leader, etc. This task is much more difficult than was Hitler's. For a start he had only one nation to work on, whereas the Profitist ethic is now worldwide. In addition Hitler had merely to prey upon all the current dissatisfactions and manipulate them to his own ends. The key to his success was that most citizens were unhappy.

In the Western world the vast majority is constantly told it is happy, or if not happy then that happiness is just around the corner. Yet we are not as happy as we could be; we know that greed, the worship of money and all it can buy, is a phoney and Q3 desire which will constantly keep us striving in a state of not quite there. In relation to all this you will already have decided whether you wish to make a significant change in yourself for yourself. Simultaneously, and without effort (see? it's not all hard work), we can go further by spreading a meditation revolution, which Swami Muktananda predicted we would see.

Reverse the mind invasion

If we want more humanity, less loneliness and aloneness, less alienation, we must...

DO SOMETHING . . .

. . . to dissolve the Profitist Zeitgeist and gradually replace it's substance with something more humanity oriented, and we must achieve this end more quickly than did Hitler in his job on the Germans. The erosion of mind and will brought about by Profitism will be slow but inevitable if progressively more people take up meditation sincerely. As more people come to know and trust and enjoy their true Selves they will like themselves better, they will exhibit and transmit the desirable Q1 changes. In doing so, they will improve the atmosphere of their surroundings at home and at work. They will be changing the energy around them.

As these changes become widespread they will start to have a positive impact on the minds and spirits of the powerful of the day. They cannot avoid it. The excesses of those in control will meet with progressively more intense non-violent opposition, including spiritual sabotage from within their own organisations – the only form of non-violent protest they cannot ignore or resist. People within brutally Profitist organisations will come progressively to reject or undermine their bosses' more outlandish requirements. This is not wishful thinking; it will happen automatically as more and more people meditate and thereby come to reap all the benefits arising therefrom.

And remember: you can keep all your Q2 fun; just cut down on the Q3.

Why do you think the Chinese communofascists, those on whom all nations now fawn, are so violently opposed to the Falun Gong? Because they are fully aware, thank you very much, of the potential power of meditation to loosen their grip on the consciousness of the citizenry. At least our ignorant leaders are not awake up to that.

Meditation downside?

Unless you count time spent on the practice, there is no downside to meditation. So far I've mentioned two possibilities and dismissed both. Meditation is not sissy and effeminate, and it does not turn you into someone you will not recognise. Another possibility is that meditation might make us too trusting, too naïve to recognise or try to counter anti-Human Values activities by the powerful of the day. In fact, meditation makes us simultaneously more alert and more courageous. In the face of threats to the wellbeing of the society you will be more likely than now to stand up and say, as George Bush was fond of saying: bring it on! Meditation can generate the Ghandi-consciousness of the twenty first century.

Desirable change

As you continue your meditation practice you will develop progressively stronger and more frequently experienced Q1 qualities such as those listed earlier. Let's look at some again.

> *contentment, joy, peace, courage, generosity, cheerfulness, faithfulness, self knowledge, loyalty, light-heartedness + any others you would like to add.*

Gavin Sinclair

As you diminish your reliance on Q2 and, particularly, Q3 preoccupations and pursuits, imagine how and how much your attitude could change in relation to the slow unfolding of a more Human Values oriented society. Let's also look at these again. Do you think it is possible for our society to move in the following direction?

emphasis on community

equality of access to the law;

equality before the law;

police power serving the majority;

genuine efforts to diminish the effects of sexism, racism and

ageism;

honesty and straightforwardness in dealings;

adequate food for all;

adequate shelter for all;

adequate and affordable health care;

educational opportunities;

security in employment;

equality of work opportunity;

caps on the fruits of greed and avarice;

respect for heritage;

unselfconscious and unforced encouragement of the value of love, peace, courage, generosity, understanding and empathy; and

knowledge itself having intrinsic value.

Suppose fifty per cent of the population, or even twenty five per cent, felt like adding, and decided to add, and *did* add a daily meditation practice to *everything else they do*. As they grew in Self knowledge, and as Q1 gradually came to replace Q3 in their lives, can you imagine how uncomfortable they would progressively find a society continuing to manifest the following:

indifference to community, emphasis on the individual inequality before the law;

police powers increasing against Human Values;

sexism, racism and ageism;

dishonesty and sneakiness in dealings;

under-nourishment and hunger;

widespread homelessness;

poor health because of lack of funds;

educational inequality bred of wealth or lack of it;

insecurity in employment;

unemployment at any level;;

exploitation of the young for profit

excessive funnelling and accumulation of wealth, where this precludes exercise of Q1 values;

indifference to or contempt for heritage;

hate and violence; cowardice; meanness in spirit and action; indifference to suffering; manipulation and exploitation for gain; ill will; an endless focus on the lowest possible denominator and the pursuit of knowledge only if it has immediately obvious practical value?

As we become more aware that each of us makes, through our actions and inactions, an essential contribution to the kind of society in which we live, so will we come to realise that we have a potential for change that goes beyond simply raising the 'good feeling' levels. The changes we seek must evolve as spirituality gains a foothold within the Zeitgeist.

By osmosis, self growth nourishes growth in others

Here is the simple beauty of the approach I am advocating. In a life incorporating Self-focused meditation, in doing your best to improve yourself and your life – however you choose to define 'improve' – you will automatically, and without any additional work on your part, be making your contribution to the changing Zeitgeist. As the commercials for unaffordable credit say, how easy is that? I suspect this is what the great teachers mean when they say that our responsibility is to change ourselves and not to try to change others *in any way*. They will be as resistant to any lecturing efforts as are we when people try to change us. It is the energy created by the sum of all the changing parts, all the people meditating with love and purpose, which will dissolve Profitism back to an appropriate level of influence, whatever level and nature that turns out to be. All we have to do is surrender to our divine inner Self and God will show the way, one by one and collectively.

As more people meditate, and step by step make contact with the Self; as they find Human Values more intrinsically attractive, and economic rationalism less so, the most unlikely people will come to see and then to deplore the devastating environmental, social and psychological consequences of existing beliefs and practices. Even tiny amounts of increasing awareness, consciousness, will bring about massive changes in emphases. As the number of meditators increases they will get together informally, symbiotically, serendipitously and deliberately. God knows what will come out of all that, but it will be good and it will be lasting.

GLOSSARY

Some terms carried over from <u>Become happy...Stay happy</u>

attachment   Liking or disliking someone or something to the point where we could not let go of that liking or disliking, or would find it very difficult to do so.

conscience   Guidance from within, not necessarily in words, which lets us know, with absolute certainty, that a thought or statement or action is or would be detrimental to spiritual progress.

C1   Conservatism which seeks to retain and protect everything that enhances Human Values

C2   Conservatism obsessed with the changing sexual mores.

C3   Reactionary, right wing conservatism, based on the authoritarian might-is-right assumption, supported by my-country-right or-wrong puffery.

ego   The sum of all tendencies of thought and action which keep us from recognising the Self within.

G love   The love that *is* God – a more accurate reference than 'God's love' or 'the love of God'.

God   The universal consciousness that creates, sustains and destroys everything that is.

karma	Action and the consequences of action. Positive and negative karmas are accumulated over many lifetimes. The purpose of spiritual practice is eventually to eliminate all karma.
liberation	See realisation.
maya	Sanskrit for illusion: the alluring and imposing reality which surrounds us all, all the time, and which, with the help of the ego, most of us assume is the only reality.
meditation	While awake, any consciously undertaken activity that silences the mind.
Q1 Quality 1	All qualities to do with purity, love and goodness: kindness, peace, contentment, joy, fearlessness, etc.
Q2 Quality 2	All qualities to do with activity, passion and worldly achievement: action, desire, excitement, stimulation, winning, etc.
Q3 Quality 3	All qualities to do with ignorance, inertia and self indulgence: uninvolved, laid back, self indulgent, prefers to stay ignorant, etc.
realisation	When all our karmas are burnt off, the final merging with universal Consciousness, God.
reincarnation	The doctrine that all humans and animals have souls, and through accumulating and demolishing *karma*, return to earth for many, many lifetimes.
	When all *karmas* are gone, there is no return.

samskara	Innate tendencies of thought and action, which come in with us from lifetime to lifetime, until we modify or delete them by taking appropriate action.
Self	A term for God which emphasises that God is within.
seva	Selfless service, work offered with love to God.
Siddha	A person who has left personhood behind, and has become one with God while still playing out *karma* in this final lifetime.
spirituality	An active focus on the human spirit, and developing attitudes and skills which aid development of knowledge of the spirit. Also, trying to live a life with such a focus.
Swami G	Swami Gurumayi Chidvilasananda, the head of Siddha Yoga worldwide and my Guru.
unmesha	The flashing forth of spiritual insights.
Yoga = union	a. A spiritual discipline, aimed at achieving insight and tranquillity.
	b. A system of exercises practiced as part of the Hindu discipline to promote control of the body and mind.

Gavin Sinclair

DEDICATION AND ACKNOWLEDGEMENTS

This book is dedicated to our world and to every living thing on and within it. It has emerged from my spiritual experiences since 1986 with Siddha Yoga and my Guru, and from my knowledge of psychology and lifelong development of personal and political convictions. I have made a possibly imperceptible effort to curb my biases and to present persuasive evidence and argument instead.

As contributors to my spiritual development I wish to acknowledge Ray Miletic, Paul McInnes, Ram Butler and Siddha Yoga Swamis Shantananda, Kripananda, Anantananda, Ishwarananda, Mukundananda, Nikhilananda and Maheshananda. My absolute indebtedness is to Gurumayi, without whose guidance and support I have no life.

Countless people, books and movies have contributed to the direction of my worldly thinking, and I would particularly like to acknowledge my parents, my sisters Barb Wheeler and Mas Mearns, Andrew Graebner, Marcia Trickey, Ray Molyneux, Duncan Richards, Janie Louder, Fred Finch, Graeme Whittingham, Peter Scott, John Poole, Diana Marr, Len Mooring, Gaile Jonikis, Jim Lumsden, Heather Sinclair, Malcolm Levene, Frank Naylor, David Malloch, Gordon Hammer, Oliver Dunne, Diana Gibbs, Bill Hopes, Alex Carey, Edna Ross, Maggie Poole-Johnson.

Above all I thank my wife, Wendy (Lakshmi) Sinclair, for her thoughtful and expert editing of this book, and for being a major contributor to my personal and political maturity. If I agree with something I more than tend, automatically I hope, to absorb it and make it my own, as though I had thought of it. I know I have done this with much of Wendy's input into my intellectual life. I ask her to forgive me. Whatever I am I would be much less without Wendy as my love and best friend.

Yours fatally, Profitism

Verily, one becomes good by action,
bad by inaction.

The Upanishads

When we sit for meditation, even though it seems that
we're not doing very much, a lot is happening on the
inside. This practice is the highest form of seva, it
brings about each individual's transformation.
When you carry your inner transformation to wherever
you live and wherever you work, you are performing a
great service to humanity.

Gurumayi Chidvilasananda

You would want the whole planet in voice
and the totality of intimate human relations
composing a hymn to enlightenment
    if that were possible.

E. L. Doctorow, <u>City of God</u>

Gavin Sinclair

www.ingramcontent.com/pod-product-compliance
Lightning Source LLC
Chambersburg PA
CBHW062208280526
45788CB00001B/494